"Christopher Columbus,
Discoverer of the New World"

Detail of a painting in the map room
of the Vatican, Rome.

THE MYSTERY OF THE ANCIENT MAPS

From the same author:
- *The FBI, complice of 9/11*;
- *Geopolitics of Cryptocurrencies* (co-author: Nancy Gomez);
- *L'Arme climatique*;
- *L'Arme environnementale* (to be published).

Talma Studios
231, rue Saint-Honoré
75001 Paris – France
www.talmastudios.com
contact@talmastudios.com
Image p. 2: © Shutterstock, Shippee

ISBN: 979-10-96132-13-3

© All rights reserved

THE MYSTERY OF THE ANCIENT MAPS

Those extraordinary anomalies which question the history of humanity

Patrick Pasin

3rd edition

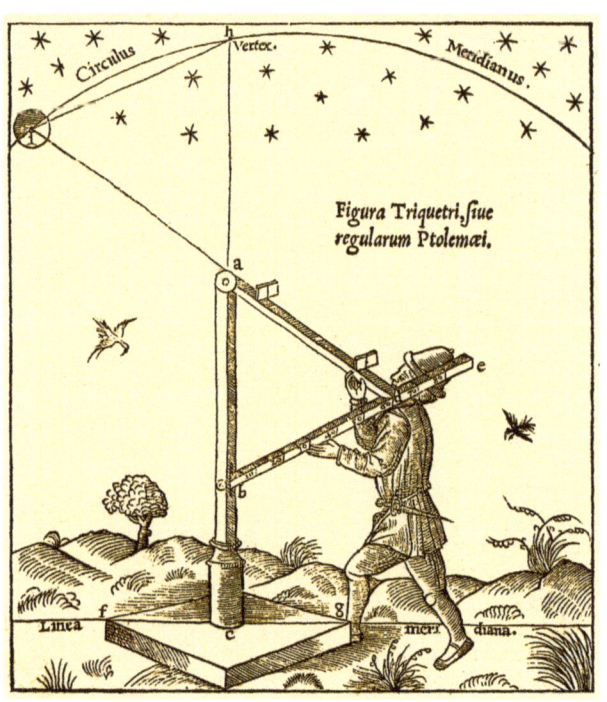

Table of Contents

	Page
Introduction	9
Chapter 1: The Arab Travelers	15
Chapter 2: Antiquity	27
Chapter 3: The First Christians	43
Chapter 4: China	47
Chapter 5: Three More Amazing Maps	53
Chapter 6: The Pre-Columbian Portolans	61
Chapter 7: After the Discovery of the New World	77
Chapter 8: Antarctica	99
Conclusion	107

*Portrait of a Man,
Said to be Christopher Columbus*
painting of Sebastiano del Piombo (1519).

Introduction

From ancient times, men began to cover distances, and oceans gradually stopped being obstacles. Their maps, namely those that survived till our time, show a fragmented representation of the Earth, because it was limited to the three known continents: Africa, Asia and Europe.

Then came the late 15th century, which constituted the major and final breakthrough: after the discovery of America by Europeans, the picture of the world was never going to be the same. Neither will the world be the same again.

To arrive at this stage, it only required a couple of years, which preceded and started the Renaissance. Thus, in less than five years was bypassed for the first time the southern tip of Africa and America was discovered. In five years, the essentials were achieved, although there will be other stages in the great maritime explorations. Here are the main ones, classified in chronological order, as taught by academic history.

1) The Circumvention of Africa

At the head of a fleet of three ships, Bartholomew Diaz left Lisbon in August 1487 to explore the African coast.

In December, he arrived at what is today known as Namibia. He continued his journey southward.
Caught in a heavy storm, he was carried by the winds from the Atlantic and became the first European traveler to cross the edge of the southern part of Africa, which was referred to as the "Cape of Good Hope" after his return.
He continued along the East coast, heading towards the North, but a riot amongst his ship crew forced him to turn back. He returned to Lisbon in December 1488, after a journey of over a year and a half.

2) The Discovery of America

It is needless going into details: everyone knows that Christopher Columbus discovered America in 1492. It is an established fact, which is indisputable and has been undisputed for a long time now.

3) The Expeditions towards the Indies

Ten years after Bartholomew Diaz, on July 8th 1497, Vasco da Gama left Lisbon to bypass Africa and reach India through the Indian Ocean. He landed in Calicut, which is today in the State of Kerala, on May 21st 1498, i.e. after ten months of journeying.
He embarked on his second trip in 1502, heading a larger fleet of twenty-one ships.
Then a third trip in 1524, but Vasco da Gama died shortly after his arrival in India, on December 24.

4) The Circumvention of America

Ferdinand Magellan, a Portuguese explorer and navigator who worked for the King of Spain, Charles I, who later became the powerful Charles V, left Seville in September 1519, and headed towards the southern part of America. The aim was to find a route through the west to reach India.

After many misadventures, such as a rebellion, shipwreck, desertion, etc., Magellan entered in October 1520 a strait which now bears his name, before circumventing what was later known as "Tierra del Fuego." He then ventured into an ocean which he named the "Pacific," due to the calmness of its waters.

The ship crew sailed northwards, towards the Indies, but Magellan never made it there: he was killed at the battle of Mactan on April 27th 1521 by the natives of that small Philippines Island.

Victoria, the last ship of the expedition, left the Moluccas archipelago, at the eastern part of Indonesia, on December 21st 1521, crossed the Indian Ocean, passing through the Cape of Good Hope, and then headed up towards Spain.

After almost exactly three years from their departure, the eighteen surviving crew members reached the province of Cádiz, on September 6th 1522, thereby becoming the first Europeans to have sailed round the world—what is now referred to as "circumnavigation."

5) The Discovery of Australia

This discovery is generally attributed to James Cook, a lieutenant in the Royal Navy, in 1770. In fact, it seemed to have been discovered by the Portuguese explorer Cristóvão de Mendonça in about 1522, i.e. two and a half centuries earlier.

The Spanish Luis Váez de Torres would have sailed off the coast of Australia in 1605, but it was the Dutch navigator Willem Janszoon who became officially known to be the first European to have landed in what is today known as Queensland (at the northeast) on February 26th 1606.

6) The Circumnavigation of America

It was not before 1741 and Vitus Bering, a Danish explorer who worked for the Russian Navy, that the Western world had proof that America and Asia were two separate continents. The strait that separates them is named after its official discoverer.

7) The Discovery of Antarctica

Officially, Captain James Cook was the first to cross the Antarctic Circle (66° 33'), on 17 January 1773. He was actually heading a little further south but, blocked by the ice, he had to turn back. He managed to descend even closer to the pole the following year, but he concluded that there was no continent, only ice as far as the eye could see.

It was not until almost four decades later, in 1820, that Antarctica was considered to have been seen for the first time —"seen," not even explored. That year, Captain Bellingshausen, of Tsar Alexander I's Navy, Captain Bransfield, of King George III's Royal Navy, and American sealer Nathaniel Palmer visited Antarctica, the first two in January and the third in November.
Although not all historians agree, it was another American sealer who first set foot on the White Continent on February 7, 1821.
Thus, according to those who write history today, Antarctica has only been known since the 19th century.

Logically, the evolution of maps should correspond to the main stages of these great maritime discoveries. It is therefore impossible to see America on a map drawned before 1492.
However, this is one of the numerous anomalies that are presented in this book. Most of which have already been pointed out by other authors who were also perplexed about the incompatibilities between these ancient maps and the chronology of events taught by academic history, but they were quickly discredited by the "official" historians. So, why not check this out on our own since many ancient maps are available on the Internet, notably via the Wikimedia Commons site?

At the beginning of the research, the maps studied did not show any anomaly, until we came across an Arabic map from the 10th century. It came as a blow, from where many more surprises followed. This led to the production of this book and the documentary titled *The Mystery of the Ancient Maps*, produced and directed by this same author.

It seems inconceivable that academic historians failed to make these observations, since these anomalies were clearly visible, just by looking at these maps.

What therefore could justify their silence?

Is it because this could not only question the great discoveries but also, in part, the history of mankind?

So what? Is it not a historian's duty to review his predecessors' errors and inaccuracies? So why not apply the same rules to such an important subject? Are they prisoners of an official "dogma" that prevents them from at least asking questions to the obvious answers given by these maps?[1]

In any case, it is now up to you to look, explore time and spaces left by our ancestors. You will not come out of this unscathed. Especially since the first subject comes like a thunderbolt out of a blue sky. And it is only the beginning.

---

1. The maps presented in this book can all be found on the Wikimedia Commons platform (https://commons.wikimedia.org) and better still, in departments and museums where they are kept.

Chapter 1

The Arab Travelers

1) Al-Masudi
Abū al-Hasan 'Alī ibn al-Husayn ibn 'Alī al-Mas'ūdī, known by the name of Al-Masudi, was born in Baghdad at the end of the 9th century and died in Egypt in 956. As a historian and geographer who had travelled extensively until Asia, he had written throughout his life, on the basis of his travels, a monumental amount of work on the history and geography of the world. Indeed, he visited Iran, Saudi Arabia, the Eastern coast of Africa, India, and many others.

Most of his books, about twenty, have been lost, but at least two still remain: *The Golden Meadows and Mines of Gems* and *The Book of the Warning and Revision*.

As we do not have any map drawn by Al-Masudi, we do not know how exactly he represented the world before the year 1000. Nevertheless, from his writings still available, here is how his understanding of Earth has been reconstituted:

As with most Arab cartographers of the time, the South was positioned at the top. Let us put the map in the North-South direction.

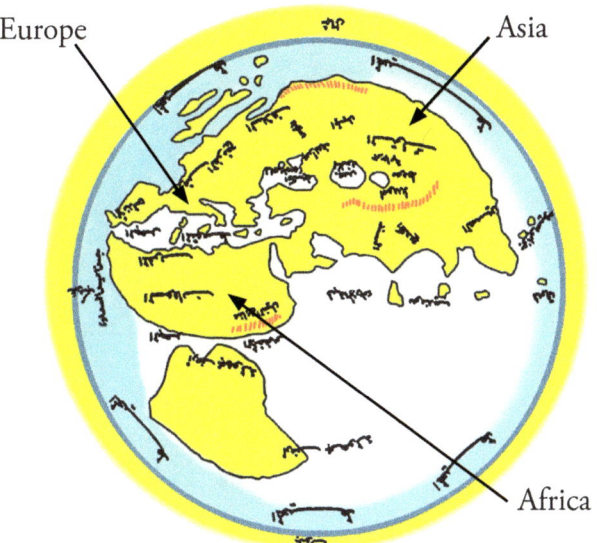

We recognize Europe, Asia, and Africa beneath the Mediterranean.

Yet, surprisingly, Al-Masudi added a fourth continent in the South, of almost the same size as Africa.

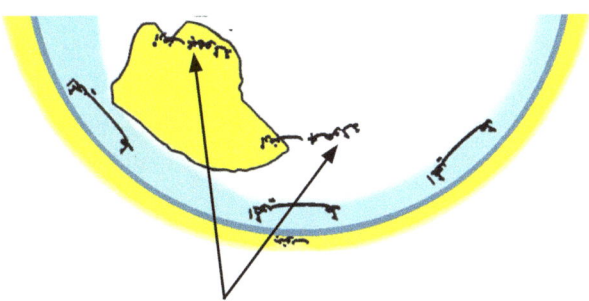

This text means "unknown land."

What could that continent be? There are only four possibilities: the Arctic, Antarctica, Australia or America. Given its position, size and shape, it cannot be the Arctic, Antarctica or Australia, which only leaves America.

Of course, the conclusion that Al-Masudi had knowledge of its existence may seem daring according to history's official discovery by Christopher Columbus five centuries later. So let us present the main text that leads to this conclusion. It comes from his book *The Golden Meadows and Mines of Gems*:

> It is a fairly widespread opinion that this sea[2] is the source of all other seas. In our book *The Historical Annals*[3], we report all the wonderful things that have been told about these lands and discuss what has been seen by the men who risked their lives to see it, some of whom have returned safe and sound, while others have perished. Thus, a resident of Spain named Khachkhach, from Córdoba, gathered a group of young people, his compatriots, and travelled with them on the Ocean in boats he had prepared. After a rather long absence, they all returned loaded with loot. Moreover, this history is known to all Spaniards.

---

2. The Atlantic Ocean.
3. This book is lost.

It was around 889 that Khachkhach made this journey, and according to Al-Masudi, he was not the only one who risked his life on the Atlantic Ocean traveling to America and coming back.

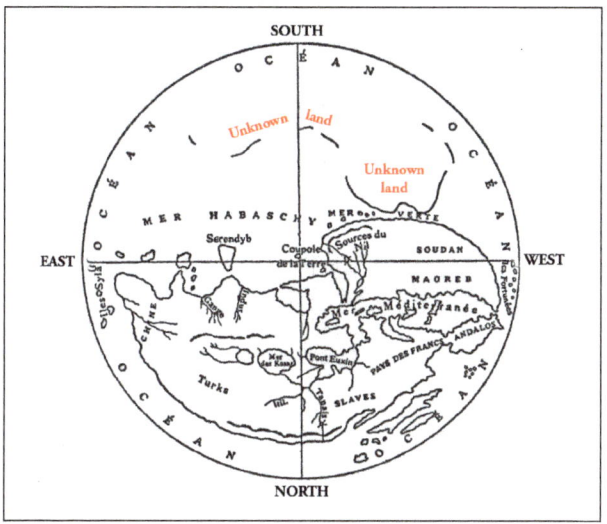

Another world map reconstituted on the basis of Al-Masudi's writings show an "unknown land."

Thus, more than a thousand years ago, the Muslim world already knew that there existed another continent in the west of the Atlantic Ocean.

2) Ibn Hawqal

Mohammed Abul-Qasim ibn Hawqal was an amazing character: he spent almost thirty years of his life traveling to Asia and Africa, between the years 943 to 969. In 977, he wrote his book *The Face of the Earth*.

Having extensively traveled through the world, here's how he described it (water is in green):

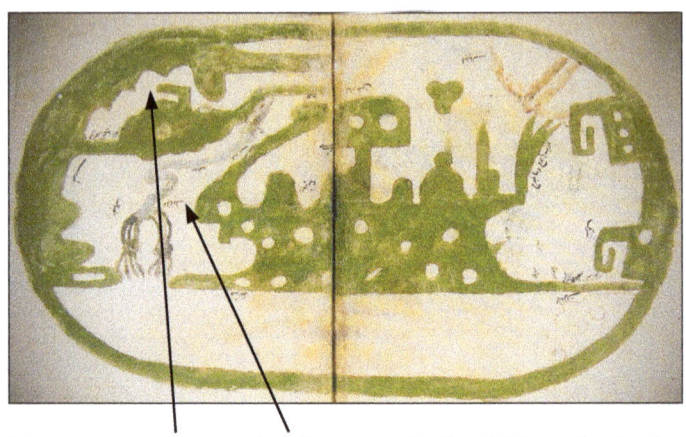

There is Europe and Africa, with the Nile, which the Muslim world already knew had several sources. There is Mecca, then the Arabian Peninsula, India, Asia with China.

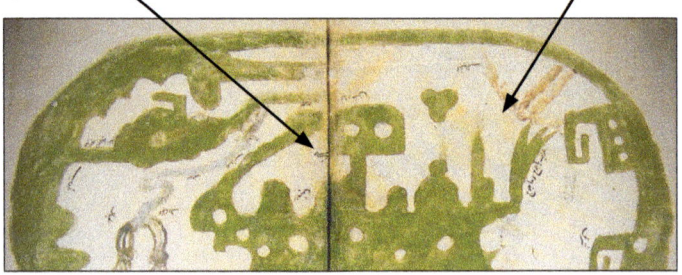

And finally, at the far end in the East, appears a continent as large as Africa. Moreover, it is independent:

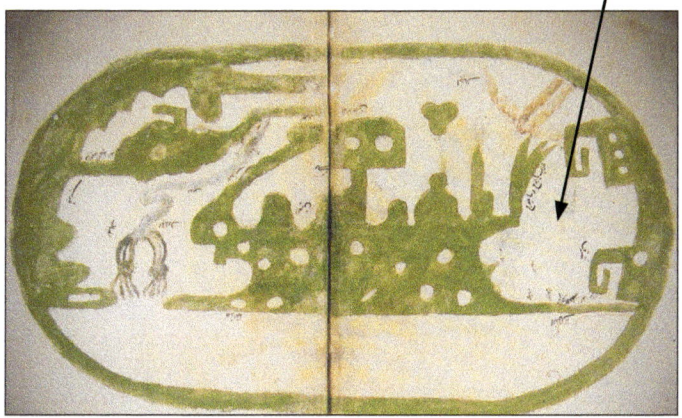

Can it be anything else but America? With today's names, we would have:

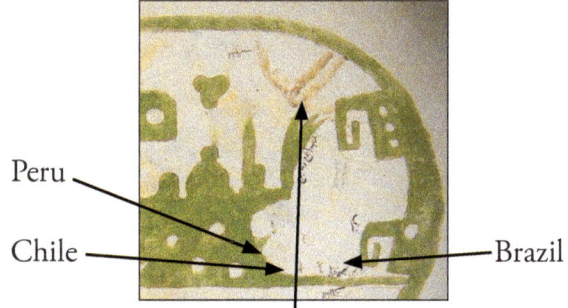

The mountains of the Kamchatka Peninsula and of eastern Siberia are the only ones represented on the map, which is surprising: although he has traveled extensively, it is difficult to imagine that Ibn Hawqal has gone to the end of the world.

We would also have:

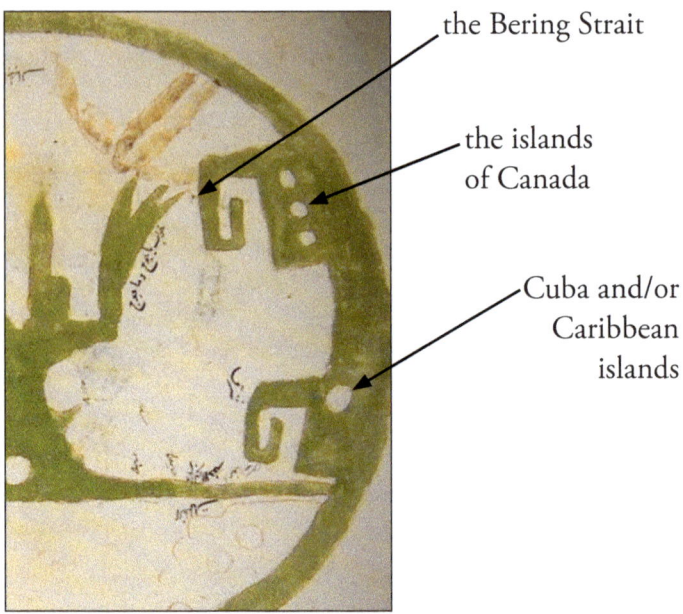

- the Bering Strait
- the islands of Canada
- Cuba and/or Caribbean islands

America represented on an Arab map of the 10th century! Isn't it amazing compared to the official history of its discovery by Christopher Columbus, five centuries later? This is further evidence that the continent was already known more than a thousand years ago.

Another surprise is this text which seems posterior. Its translation means "the ruins of Yajouj and Majouj." These are the Arab variants of Gog and Magog, the allies of evil in the *Bible*. Thus, they are located in North America!

They appear twice in the Quran, mainly in Sura 18, called "Sura of the Cave." In this Sura, a character called Dhul-Qarnayn also appears, but we do not know who he is. Some commentators speculate that he was Alexander the Great or Cyrus the Great, founder of the Persian Empire.

This name of Dhul-Qarnayn literally means "the possessor of two horns." But Ibn Hawqal drew two horns on his map. Was Dhul-Qarnayn the mysterious master of America?

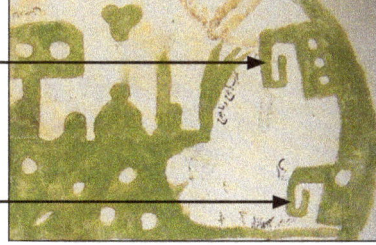

Another impossibility for that time: Ibn Hawqal drew Antarctica fairly close to modern maps.

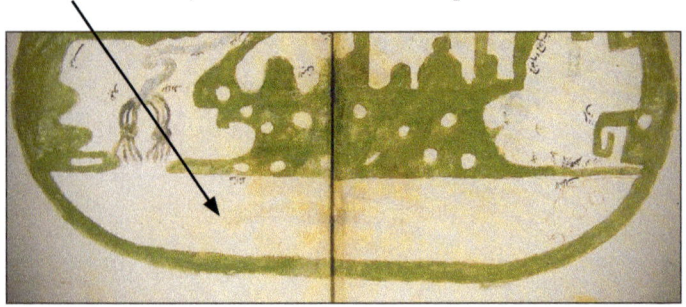

Let us recall that this continent was not supposed to have been seen until 900 years later! (see Chapter 8). Who went there at the time of Ibn Hawqal or before?

Another thing that caught our attention on comparing the writings of Al-Masudi and Ibn Hawqal, both of the 10th century, is that while Al-Masudi knew that there were lands in west of the Atlantic, Ibn Hawqal placed this continent in the east direction, as in today's maps drawn from Asia.

This implies that the two travelers did not have the same sources, but mainly that the American continent had been reached both through the Atlantic and the Pacific! This also means that the full circumnavigation of the globe had been done more than a thousand years ago, at least 500 years before Christopher Columbus' first voyage.

Not only do these maps show that the two oceans were crossed, but also that the trip around America was made, because it is detached from other continents and the southern part was pretty well drawn.

Ibn Hawqal's map presents even more surprising points, because it shows that the continent is independent from Antarctica. Also, on the contrary, he connected Africa to Antarctica, with the Nile having its source between the two continents. Thus, when this map was drawn, the trip around America had already been done, but not that of Africa! This is, of course, unbelievable. Nevertheless, it is before our eyes.

Could older maps have been used as a source, at least for Ibn Hawqal? Let us start looking for them and begin to study the maps of Antiquity.

Mohammed Abul-Qasim
ibn Hawqal

Othoman miniature of
an Armillary sphere
(16th century).

Chapter 2

Antiquity

1) Babylon

Officially, one of the earliest maps of the world that we still have is of Babylonian origin and dates from the 6th century BC.

We must say "Officially," because Ancient history has a huge surprise in store for us from a much older map. We present it at the end of the chapter.

Discovered in the South of Iraq towards the late 19th century, this Babylonian clay tablet is preserved today in the British Museum.

On this clay tablet are represented Babylon, the Euphrates, Assyria, surrounded by a circular ocean.

In addition, there are seven islands, according to the text written in cuneiform.

It is impossible to know what these islands represent exactly to the Babylonians, or even whether one of these islands is America. In any case, this map is clearly not our Arab travelers' source.

2) Anaximander

According to the Greek Eratosthenes, Anaximander was the first to draw a world map. We can reasonably assume that the opinion of Eratosthenes was justified, because he was in charge of the fabulous library of Alexandria in the 3rd century BC, which had up to 700,000 books at the time of Julius Caesar. He thus had access to all the manuscripts, or almost all those known in the Mediterranean world and beyond.

Anaximander is the first author of a map whose name has come to us. We even have a bas-relief of the Antiquity that represents him.

Living in the 6th century BC, he was a mathematician, a philosopher and a geographer, and it is said that Thales was his teacher and Pythagoras was his student.

Here is the hypothetical reconstitution of the world map according to Anaximander — "Hypothetical" since we no longer have a copy:

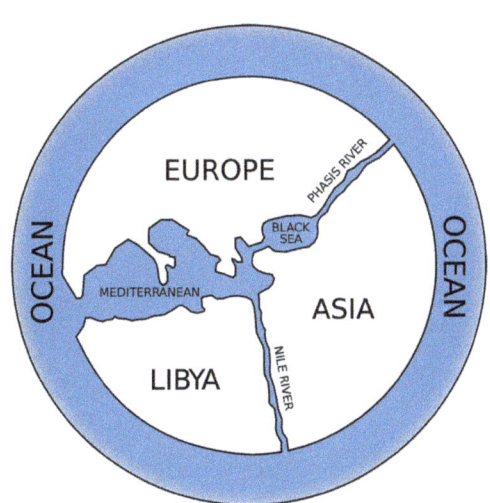

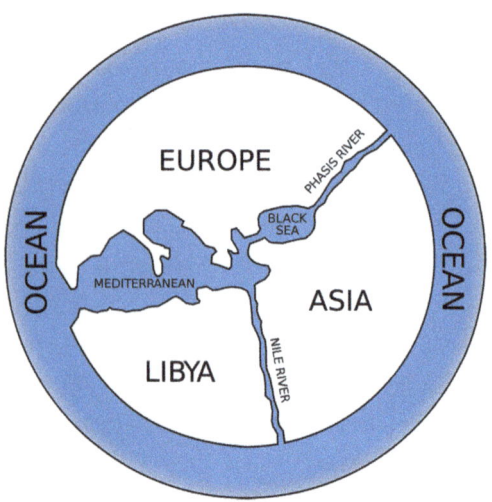

We distinguish three continents: Europe, Asia and Africa (then called "Libya"). They are separated by the Mediterranean, the Nile and the Phasis River, which is now the Don River. There is no trace of America, not even of the Poles.

Anaximander was therefore not the source for Ibn Hawqal. Nevertheless, Greek authors became inspired by his map and refined it as time went on.

Anaximander

3) Hecataeus of Miletus, Herodotus and Eratosthenes
Hecataeus of Miletus (c. 550–c. 480 BC), considered today as one of the fathers of geography, completed Anaximander's map, mainly thanks to his trips to Egypt and Asia:

As for Herodotus (c. 484–c. 425 BC), one of the fathers of history, his numerous trips enabled him to draw the world map that was known by the Greeks towards the end of the 5th century BC:

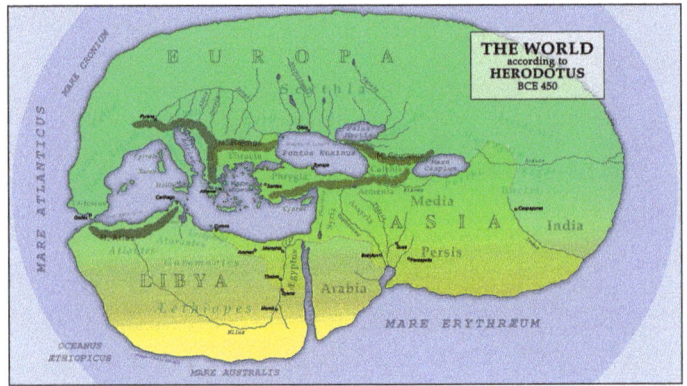

The errors are obviously numerous: the Nile, for example, does not originate from today's Atlas mountain of Morocco. However, it is only two millennia later that the various sources of the Nile were eventually known.

Let us come back to Eratosthenes, who was not only the Director of the library of Alexandria, but also an astronomer, geographer, mathematician and philosopher. One of his most stunning works was the calculation of the Earth's circumference, which he estimated to be 39,375 km. This figure is of remarkable accuracy, because the actual value is a little more than 40,000 km.

He drew a more precise map compared to those of his predecessors, because he used information that came from Alexander the Great's military campaigns, which took place right up to India.

Here is the reconstituted map, since the original one did not reach us. The origins of the Nile were better located this time:

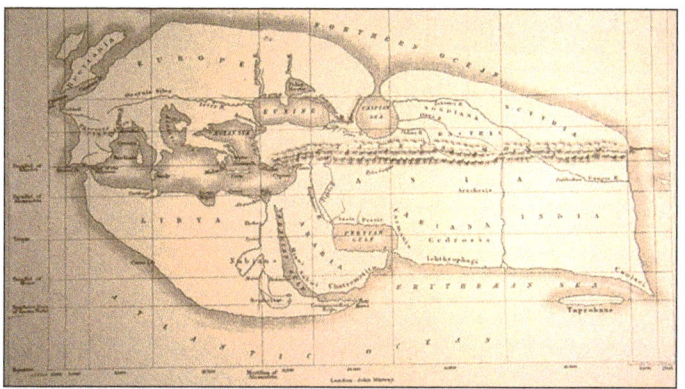

Eratosthenes was the first to have added the parallels and meridians (longitudes and latitudes), which attests to his understanding that the Earth was spherical.

Actually, what was then the shape of the Earth? The first to have concluded that it was a sphere would be Pythagoras and Parmenides, around the 5th century BC. Thus, contrary to what is often believed, the ancient world already knew that the Earth was round and not flat.

Parmenides divided the Earth into five climatic zones, which will be subsequently reproduced, like in this manuscript from the Middle Ages:

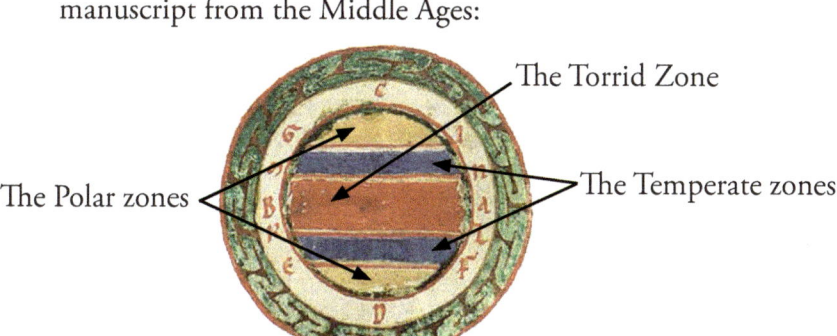

The Greeks therefore knew that the Earth was round, and as early as in the 3rd century BC, Aristarchus of Samos concluded that the Earth did not only rotate around itself, but that it also revolved around the Sun. He arrived at this conclusion almost 1,700 years before Galileo.

4) Crates of Mallus

Crates of Mallus was born in Greece around 220 BC. He was a Stoic philosopher who was famous for having built the first globe. Here is a reproduction:

The word "Œcumene" means "inhabited earth, known world."

"Antoeci" refers to those who live below the opposite latitude, therefore, in the Southern Hemisphere.

"Perioeci" refers to those who live in the same latitude but on the opposite meridian.

Crates of Mallus continued with Parmenides' idea of climatic zones and assumed that the Torrid Zone was occupied by the ocean and that the inhabited Temperate Zones are on both sides of the ocean.

And Crates of Mallus arrived at the conclusion of the existence of inhabited land to the west of the ocean. We could say he discovered America, though simply by pure reasoning. Therefore, he cannot be the source of the Arab maps. However, the idea that inhabited lands existed beyond the ocean was then injected into the Greek world.

5) Claudius Ptolemy

Then came Claudius Ptolemy, whose influence was by far the most important of the geographers of Antiquity, because it continued until the Renaissance.

A Greek astronomer and astrologer of the 2nd century AD, he is considered as one of the fathers of geography. His book entitled *Geographia* will constantly be copied for over thousand years; fortunately, since we do not have the original anymore. This copy was drawn in around the 15th century, from the hundreds of records contained in *Geographia*:

This map reveals many errors, as well as many curiosities. Firstly, we notice that the Indian Ocean, known by the name "Mare Indicum," forms an inland sea, such as the Mediterranean. Strangely, it is bordered by land to the South, which could correspond to the Antarctic, which is believed to be unknown at the time.

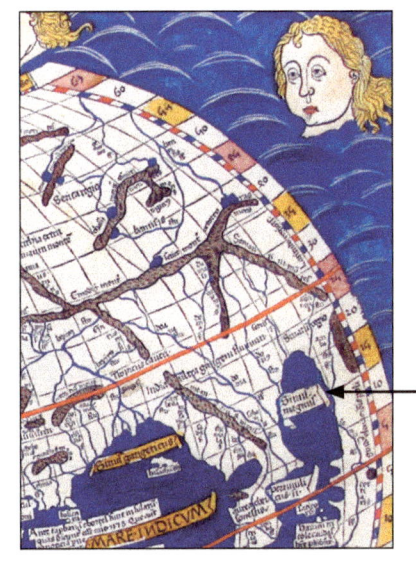

What is even more strange is the fact that Ptolemy included land on the other side of the Pacific, called "Sinus Magnus" or "Great Gulf." However, across the Pacific, there is America! He linked it to Asia, and even drew mountains to the West, as if he knew of the existence of the Andes Mountains. But he did not show how far to the East this land extended, which could have enabled us to determine which land was represented and to be able to conclude whether Ptolemy was the source for the Arab maps and texts. It seems nevertheless unlikely since Ibn Hawqal drew a continent that is independent of Asia.

6) The Peutingerian Table

Julius Caesar's adopted son Augustus, became the first Roman Emperor in 27 BC. It was under his reign that the "cursus publicus" was created, the post service that ensured officials and administrative changes within the Empire. This was strategically important for the administration of the Roman provinces as well as the army: it relied on a huge network of pathways and stages that continued to grow with the power of Rome.

We know this today thanks to a special document entitled "The Peutingerian Table." Only a single copy remains, and it was discovered in 1494 in a German library, and then given to a humanist and lover of antiques by the name of Konrad Peutinger, from whom it derived its name "Tabula Peutingeriana" or "The Peutingerian Table."

This copy seems to have been made in the 13th century by an anonymous monk. The original was made at least in the 4th century because the city of Constantinople, named in 330, was mentioned in it. The western part had disappeared but it was reconstituted thereafter.

The Peutingerian Table is extraordinarily large in size: it has a length of over 6.80 meters and consists of twelve scrolls!

It is also remarkable because it represents 200,000 km of roads, with at least 555 cities and 3,500 other place names. It thus covers the whole of the Roman Empire, the Middle East and extends to India. Who could achieve such a wonder across three continents?

The map ends in the East, with India and the Ganges:

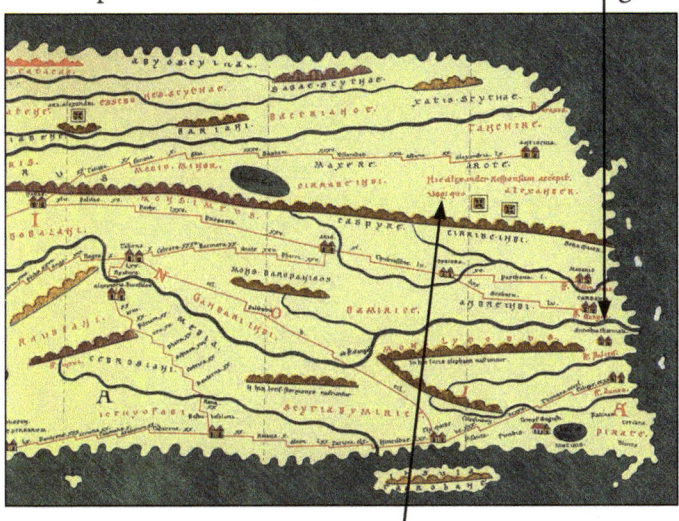

Further north, there is a nameplate on which, according to legend, Alexander the Great made write: "Alexander stopped here." It marked the limit of the known world.

The Peutinger Table could also have marked the end of our journey into Ancient history, where, with the exception of Ptolemy, which is already remarkable and adds to the mysteries of ancient maps, we did not find any trace of America there. However, a final map of Egyptian origin remains to be seen, because it is quite simply unbelievable. In the meantime, let us take a look at the remarkable Peutinger map on the next two pages.

Note: this map is too long to be contiguously presented in this book. As from the next two pages, you should therefore try to imagine the four bands, one after the other, from East to West.

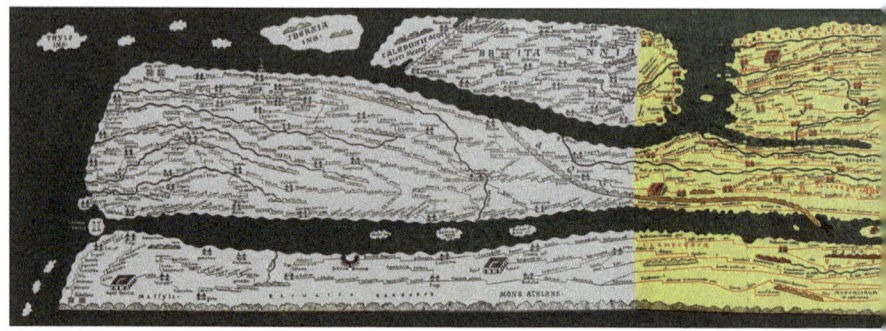

The western part of the map had to be reconstituted, in white here.

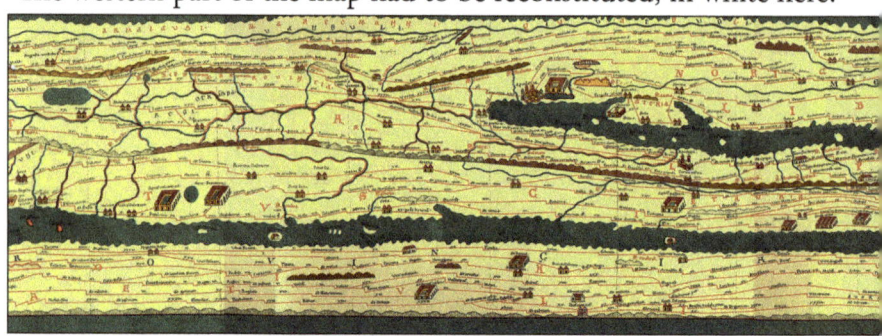

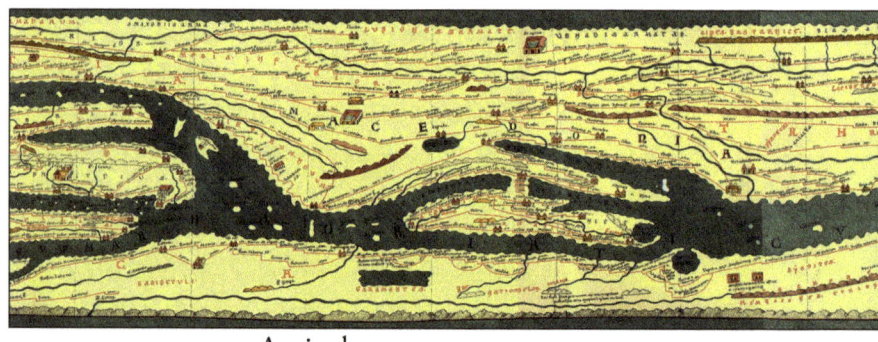

Antioch

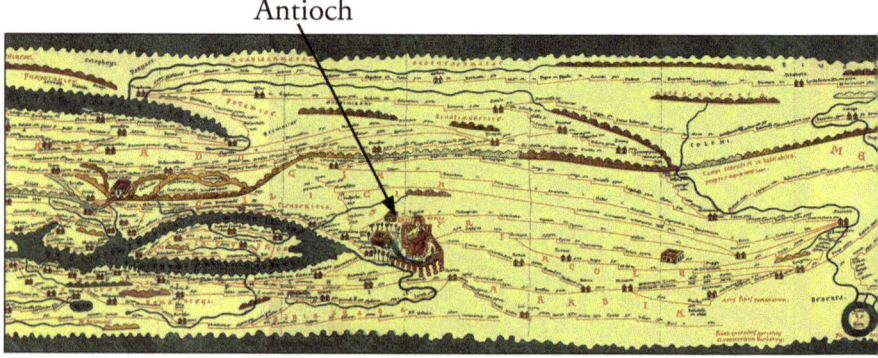

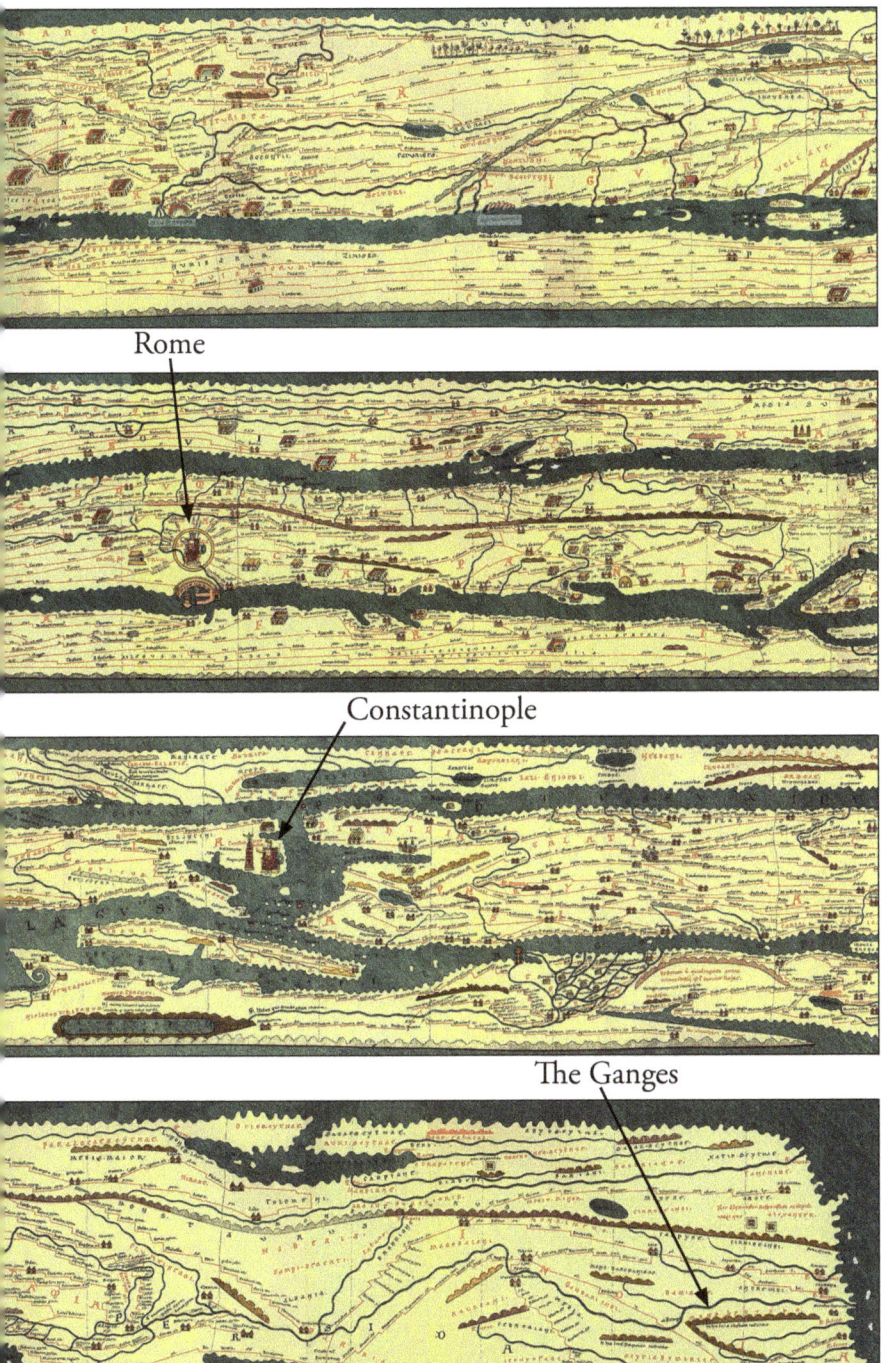

7) The tomb T100 of Hierakonpolis

This map is a reproduction of a mural painting discovered in 1898-99 in Tomb T100 at the site of Nekhen (or Hierakonpolis, for the Greeks), in southern Egypt. It is dated 3,500 years BC. The tomb has disappeared, but paintings are kept in the Egyptian Museum in Cairo.

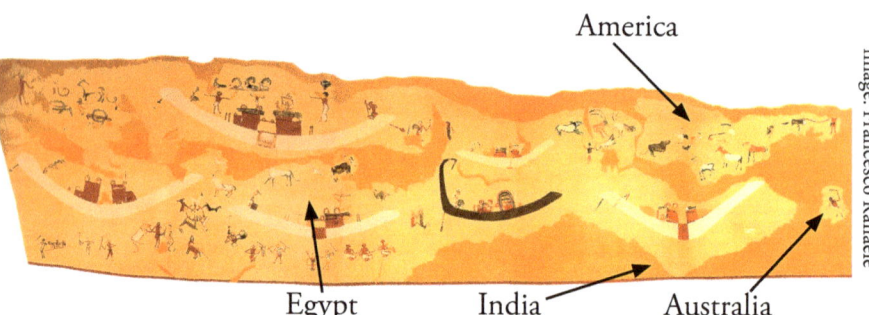

Image: Francesco Raffaele

It shows America to the east, as on Ibn Hawqal's map. The author knew that the continent was not linked to Asia since it included the current Bering Strait. He added Australia, although officially discovered about... five millennia later. Its source remains mysterious.

This proves that the Egyptians had known of America for a long time, because this mural is dated about **five thousand years** before the arrival of Christopher Columbus. Obviously, they had also circled around it. Neither Arab travelers nor other ancient cartographers had ever seen it, as it was a painting found inside a tomb. There is no doubt, however, that this knowledge was shared and had been passed down through the ages, at least in this part of the world. Until the Christians?

Chapter 3

The First Christians

1) Augustine of Hippo

Let us now have a look at the Christian maps of the world. They have some surprises for us. Let us start with Augustine of Hippo (354-430 AD), one of the four Fathers of the Catholic Church. Here is how he represented the world:

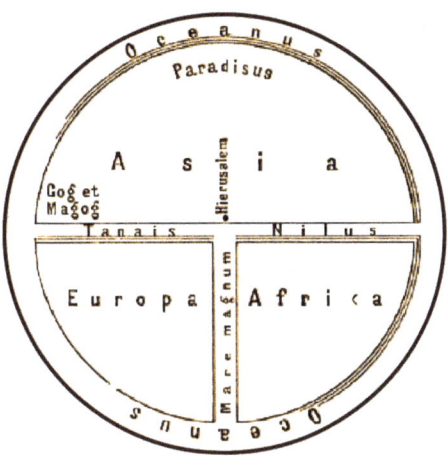

Asia is the sum of Europe and Africa. The continents are separated by the Mediterranean, the Nile and the Don River, called "Tanais." Jerusalem is at the center. Gog and Magog, the allies of evil, are in Asia. Paradise is located in the east, up on this reproduction.

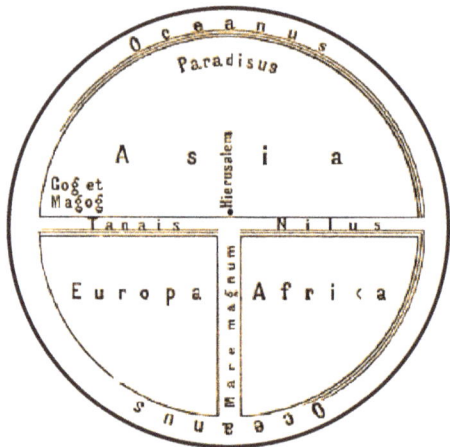

America is still far away.
Saint Augustine admitted the principle of the roundness of the Earth, but he rejected the possibility of people living in antipodes.
Obviously, he could not have been the source of the Arab travelers.

Three versions of the map, including an Arabic manuscript

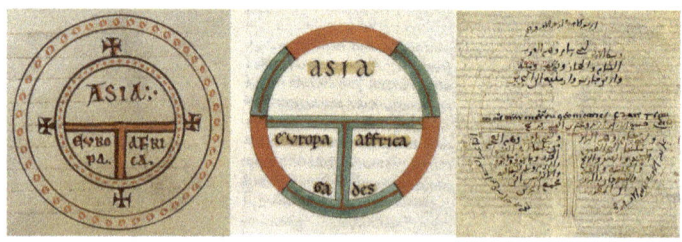

2) Beatus

In 776, the Spanish monk Beatus wrote a book entitled, *Commentary on the Apocalypse*. The original has disappeared, but there are still some thirty editions and versions that were published during the four centuries that followed. This book presents a world map:

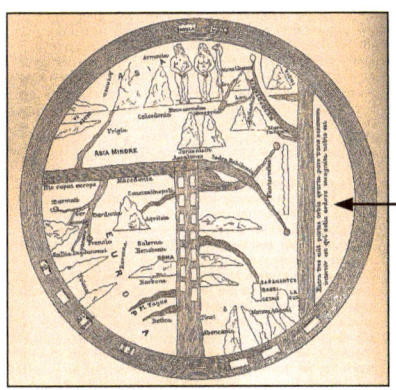

There are still three continents, i.e. Europe, Asia and Africa. But, surprisingly, Beatus added a fourth continent to the East.

The Latin text[1] says that "in addition to the three parts of the Earth, there is a fourth beyond the inner ocean, where the heat of the sun is unknown to us."

---

1. "Extra tres aut partes orbis quarta pars trans oceanum interior est qui solis ardore incognita nobis est."

It is not possible to know what that continent is —it could be America, Australia or even Antarctica—, and from where did this mysterious knowledge originate.

This book will have a profound influence on the Christian world for four centuries, but the contours of the fourth continent were too imprecise to believe that Beatus could have been the source for Ibn Hawqal two centuries later.

It is perhaps the contrary that happened: indeed, according to most historians, Beatus was born in Andalusia, then under the domination of the Arabs. Did he hear about this fourth continent beyond the Ocean from them? What other source could he have as Christians at that time barely started to talk about islands in the Atlantic Ocean and not of another continent? And they would continue to reproduce the world with only three continents for centuries.

Two other versions of Beatus' map

Chapter 4

China

China too had its cartographers. Let us see if there are traces of America on this side of the world. After all, there is just an ocean to cross.

1) The Ming map
It is under the Ming dynasty, from 1368 to 1644, that this map was designed, without any precision as to the exact year:

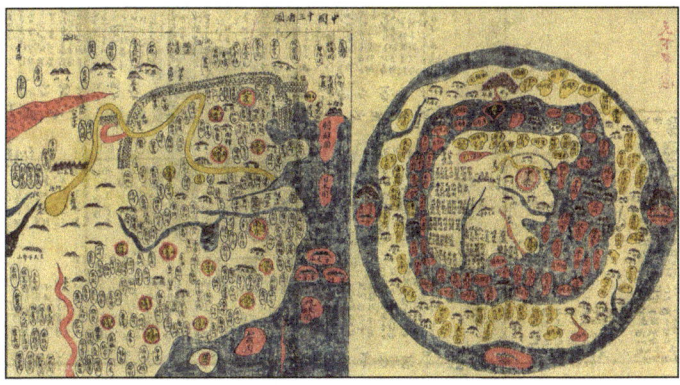

The left side represents China, while the one on the right represents the world.

It closely resembles the European medieval maps we know. Even the Red Sea is painted red. Could this map be a copy of a European map?

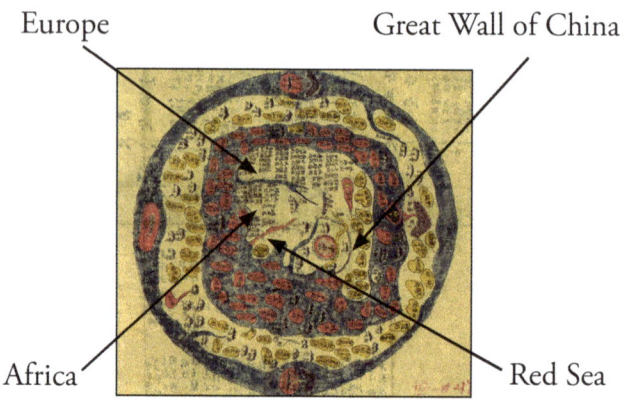

However, what differentiates them is the strip of land around the world on the Chinese map. What is it? The East and West coasts of America and the Arctic and Antarctica?

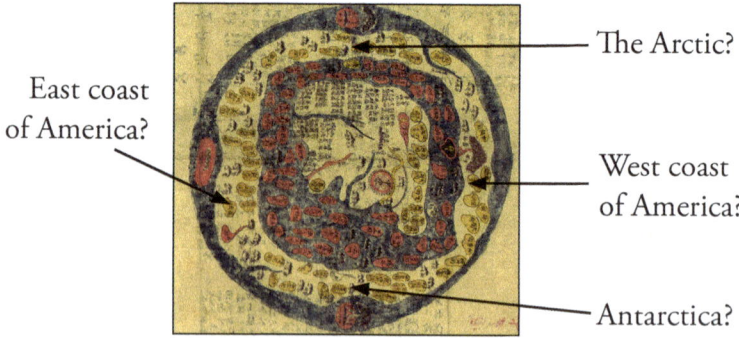

2) The Zheng He map

Legendary Chinese admiral, Zheng commanded seven maritime expeditions from 1405 to 1433 to East Africa and the Arabian Peninsula. Discovered in 2005, this map dates to 1763 but it would be a reproduction of an old map of 1418 that belonged to Zheng He:

All continents are represented, including America, Australia and Antarctica. The accuracy is impressive, but this map is considered a fake. Even if the Chinese knew America well before Columbus —we will show it later—, the slightly earlier or later Chinese maps that we studied do not seem compatible with this supposed map of Zheng He (see next page). So it probably is a fake, or at least not a map of 1418.

The Da Ming
Hun Yi Tu map
1389

Map of
the World
1470

The Sancai
Tuhui map
1607

3) The Sihai Huayi Zongtu map
This Chinese map dated 1532 is worth studying carefully:

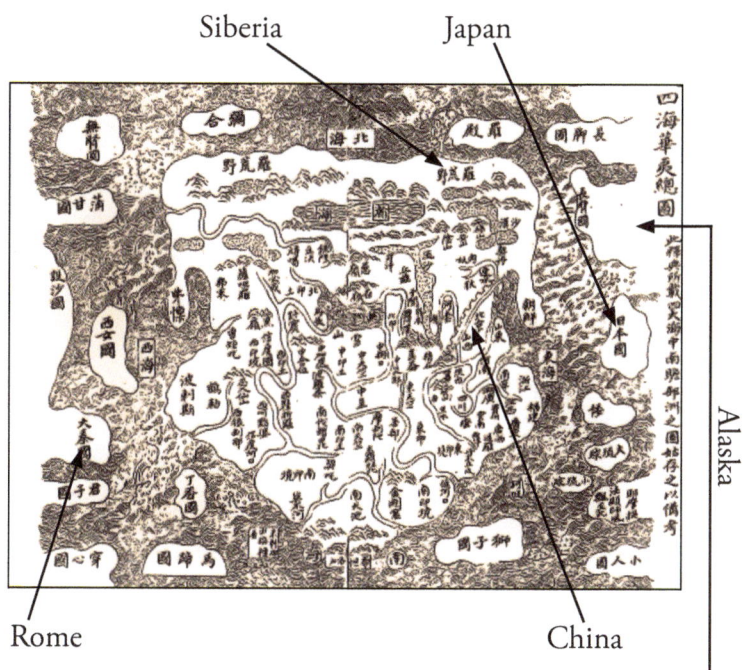

Opposite Asia, on the other side of the ocean, there is a land. Obviously, it looks like Alaska and the west of the American continent.

But it is only in the 18th century, two and a half centuries later, that the Europeans discovered Alaska. For example, it was still unknown on the 1670 map of the Dutch cartographer Frederik de Wit:

Therefore, the Chinese knew this part of the American continent centuries before the Europeans.

Chapter 5

Three More Amazing Maps

1) The Viking map of Vinland
This map was offered to Yale University in the United States by a former student more than fifty years ago.
Meant to reproduce a thirteenth century original, it is considered the first known depiction of the coast of North America on a map. The Vikings had indeed arrived in the New World more than two hundred years before Columbus.

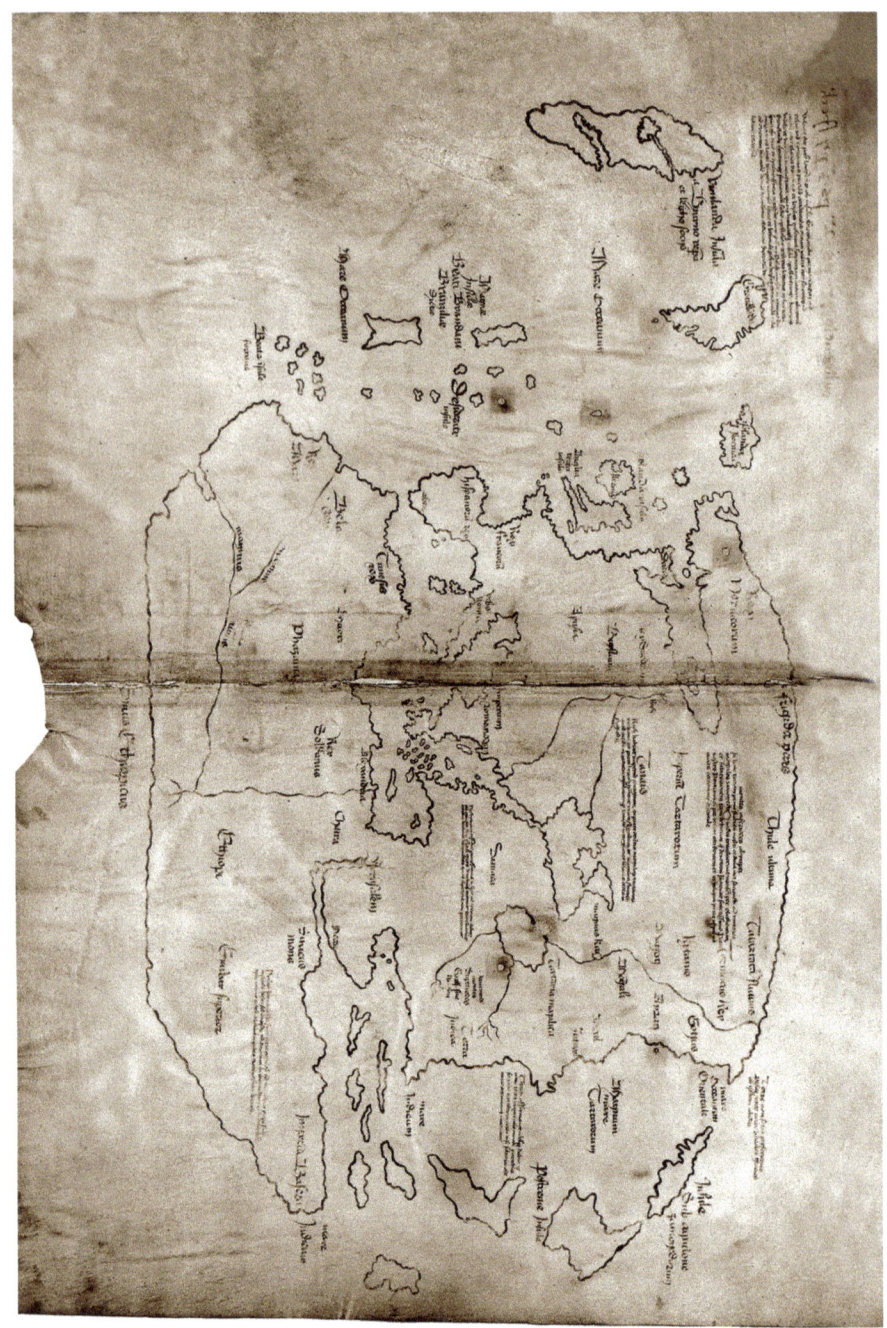

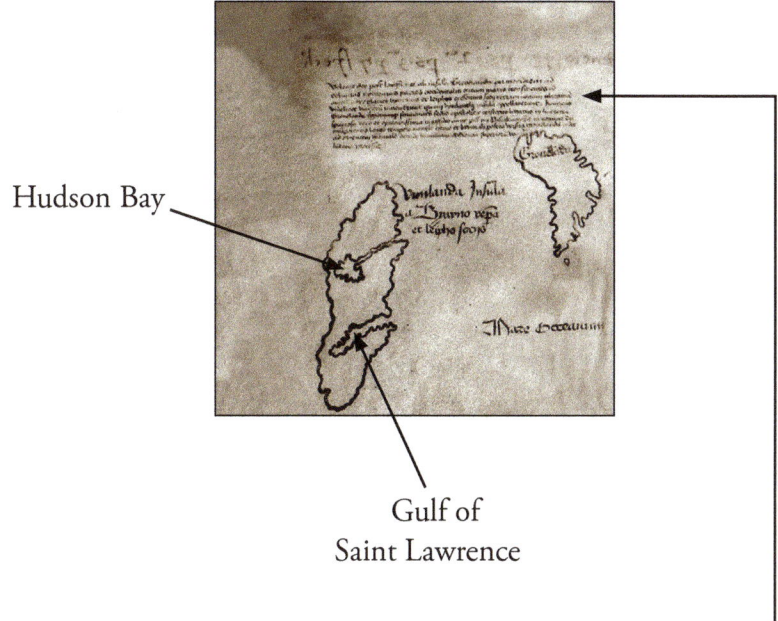

Hudson Bay

Gulf of
Saint Lawrence

The legend at the top left says: "By God's will, after a long voyage from the island of Greenland to the south toward the most distant remaining parts of the western ocean sea, sailing southward amidst the ice, the companions Bjarni and Leif Eriksson discovered a new land, extremely fertile and even having vines [...] which island they named Vinland."

There are other surprises on this map, mainly an island in the west of the Atlantic almost as large as England named as "Branziliæ." Obviously, it makes us think of Brazil, although this is supposed to be impossible.

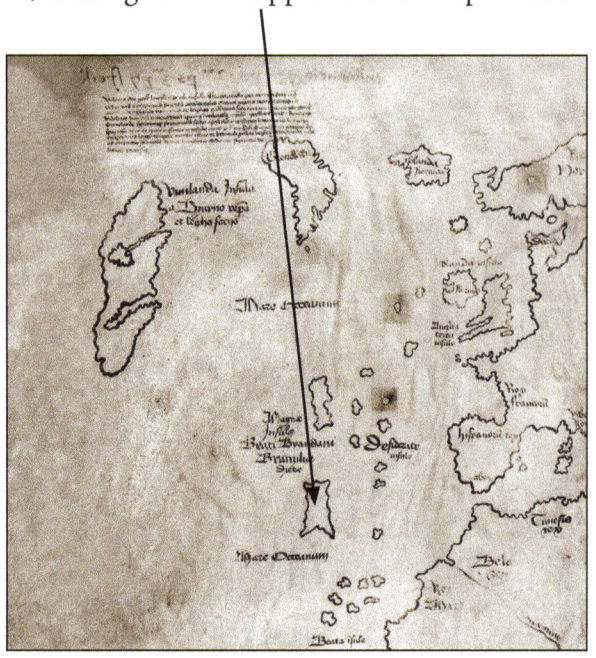

Studies consider that this map is a fake. However, archeology has confirmed that the Vikings had established a colony on the coast of what is now Canada, about 500 years before Columbus. So why would they not have drawn a map, whether this one or another, anyway? And why would they have not gradually descended further down the continent?

2) The map of Lucas Brandis

In any case, the Nordic sagas will inspire the Medieval West, at least until the 15th century and this map of Lucas Brandis, a German typographer and editor.

Made in 1475 and presented in the monumental history of the world entitled *Rudimentum Novitiorum*, it was the first printed world map — Gutenberg invented the printing press some twenty years prior to that time.

This Lucas Brandis map held a major surprise for us: indeed, a little piece of America is drawn above, since it represented the Vinland therein. This was achieved some seventeen years before Christopher Columbus' first voyage!

3) Marco Polo

In 1935, Marcian Rossi, a retired merchant, offered a map to the Library of Congress of the United States, which he said came from an ancestor friend of Marco Polo. It would have belonged to Marco Polo himself and therefore dates back to the 13th century.

The FBI conducted analyses with ultraviolet rays from 1943 on and discovered that there are three levels of ink which means that three drawings were superimposed.

We recognize Asia on the left, Alaska and the coast of North America to the right. The Aleutian Islands, which form a semi-circle of 1,900 km (1,200 mi), are even represented.

The names of the places are written in Arabic. There are also Chinese characters on two columns and a Venetian text.

So, even if this map did not belong to Marco Polo and he did not go to America, it is, nevertheless, further evidence that the continent was known in Asia for centuries before 1492. It would make sense, since only a little over 80 km separates Asia and America via the Bering Strait.

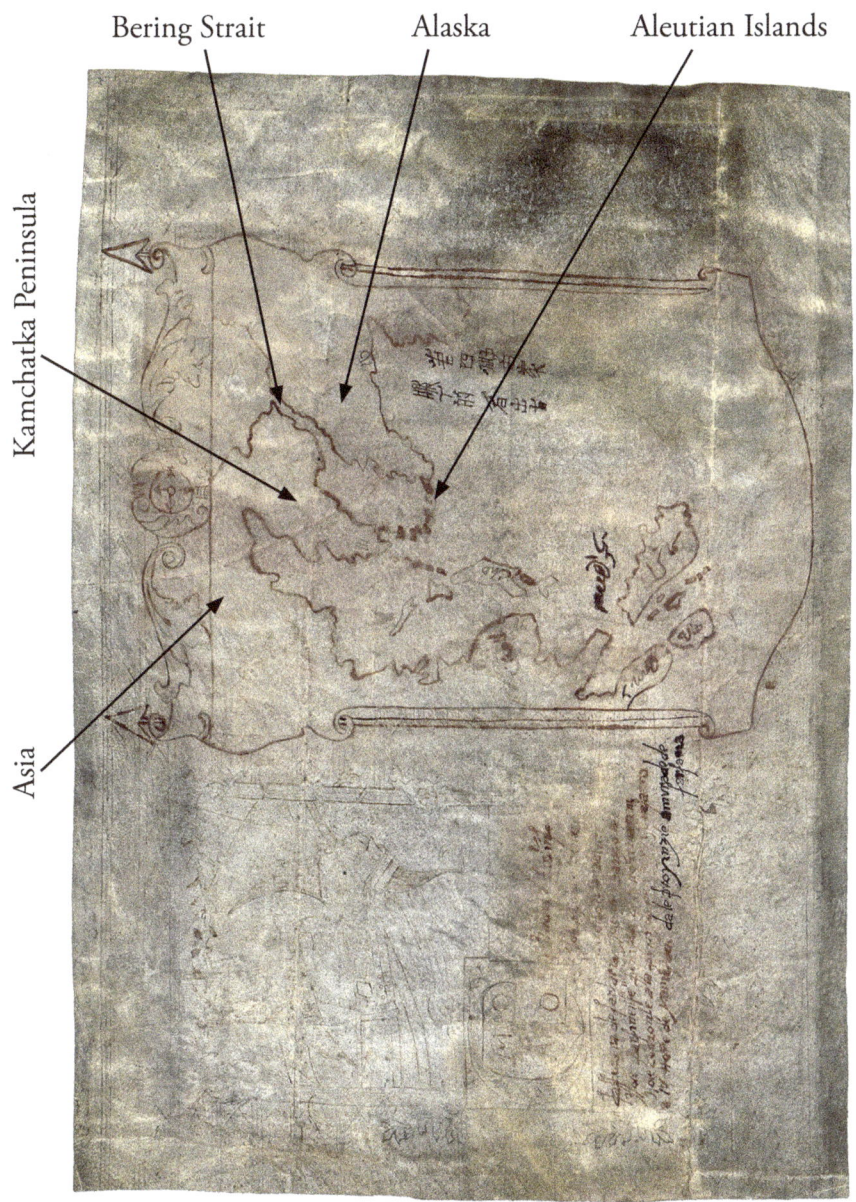

An example of a portolan chart
(14th century)

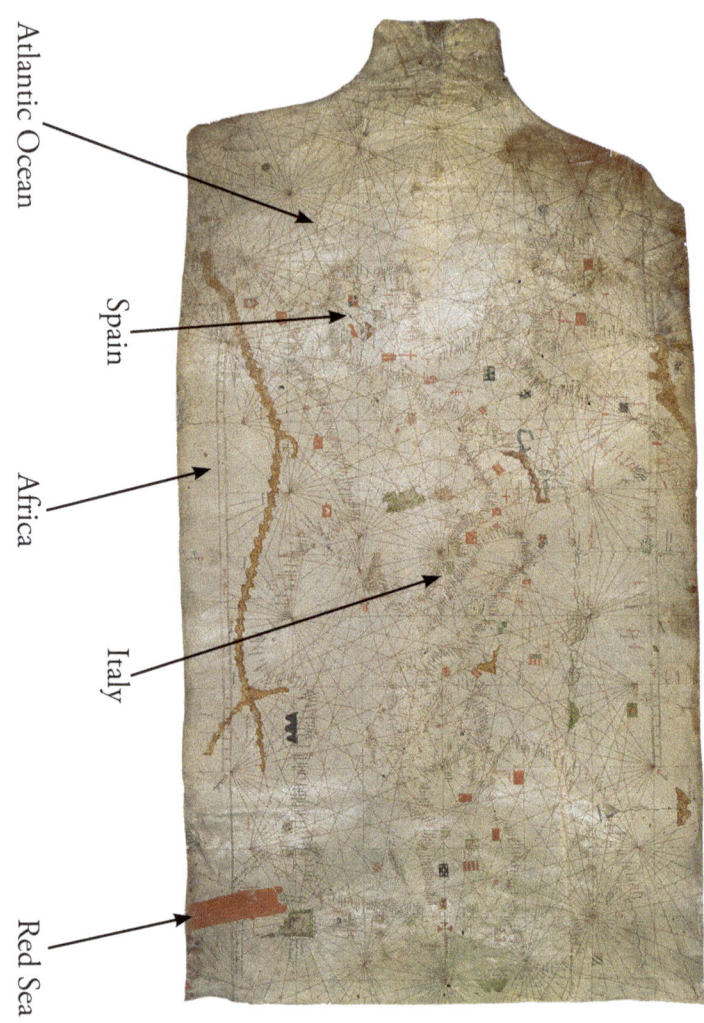

Chapter 6

The Pre-Columbian Portolans

It was also well before the arrival of Christopher Columbus that Portolans charts began to appear. These were marine charts for navigation. They located ports, the dangers that surrounded them, currents, winds, etc. The outlines of the coasts were represented by names.
What is surprising is the accuracy with which these maps were drawn at that time.
Major maritime kingdoms like Spain and Portugal considered portolan charts as state secrets. This is all the more understandable as islands are beginning to appear west of the Atlantic that are supposed, according to official history, to have not yet been discovered.
As these anomalies seriously contradict the dogma of the discovery of America by Christopher Columbus, modern day historians explain that these islands were 'imagined', 'fantasized', 'phantom islands' and other similar qualifiers.
Thereby, they ignore the maps drawn by the monk Beatus (8th century onwards) and, of course, the Arab texts and maps that we presented in the first chapter.
They will probably retort that Occident had no knowledge of them. It is possible, but this would mean forgetting the

long presence of the Crusaders and Knights of the Temple across the Mediterranean, as well as all exchanges that led to disseminate Arab science in Europe, including algebra with... Arabic numerals, not to mention the presence of Muslims in Spain up to the 15th century.

It will also mean forgetting the trips across the Atlantic, such as the one made by the Irish monk Saint Brendan of Clonfert, at about 544-545 AD. Back in Ireland, he claimed to have discovered an island, which he compared to paradise. Today it is understood that he reached the Azores, the Caribbean or even Cuba.

The "Brendan Island" or "Saint Brendan's Island" then appeared regularly on maps until the one drawn in 1570 by Abraham Ortelius, a geographer and cartographer from Antwerp.

I. Brazil
1) Angelino Dulcert

One of the oldest portolan charts we still have was designed by the Spanish cartographer Angelino Dulcert in 1339.

The outlines are fairly precise and latitudes and longitudes are surprisingly accurate for the time. But even more surprisingly, he mentioned an island called "Brasil," off the coast of Ireland.

At the southern part of the Atlantic, he added the St Brendan's Island.

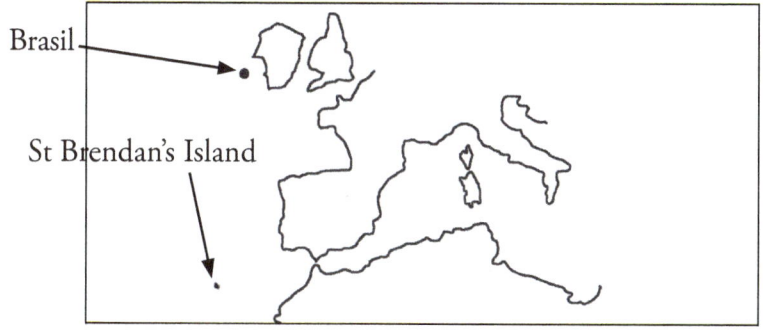

2) The Pizzigani Brothers

Some thirty years later, in 1367, the island of "Brazir" appeared on the map of the brothers Domenico and Francisco Pizzigani, Venetian cartographers. It was even mentioned in three different areas:

This map gives the impression that the Pizzigani Brothers collected testimonies from sailors who located "Brazil" in different locations, but since they could not imagine that it was a continent, they positioned islands at the corresponding locations. They even added the St Brendan's Island. Of course, it would mean that the crossing of the Atlantic took place at least 125 years before Columbus.

On this part of the map, around the "Brazir Insula," it is talked about dragons attacking men. Obviously, some people did not want everyone to visit that part of the Atlantic and its riches.

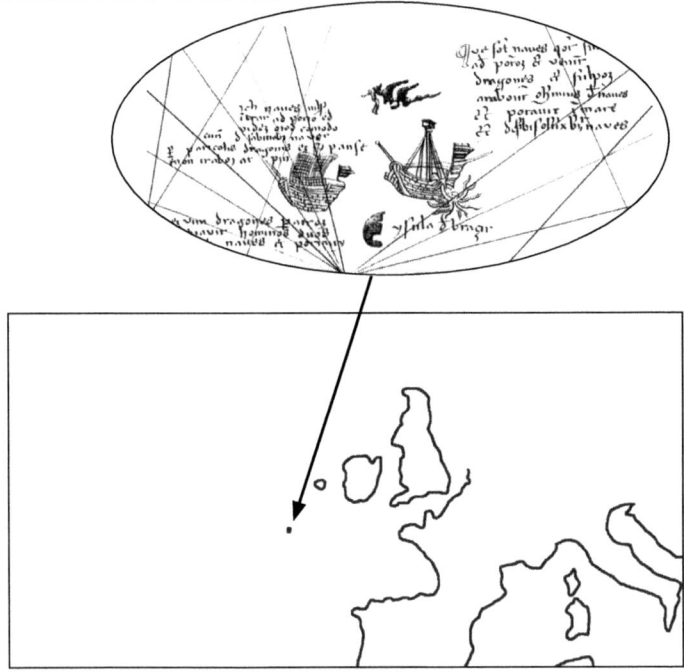

3) The Catalan Atlas

Eight years later, in 1375, on the gorgeous "Catalan Atlas" of Abraham Cresques, a cartographer from the School of Majorca, the island of Brazil or "Insula de Brazil" appeared again in the Atlantic Ocean, but on two spots:

Insula de Brazil

4) Guillem Soler

About him, we do not know much, except that he was a Christian and cartographer from the School of Majorca, as were Angelino Dulcert and Abraham Cresques. He designed this portolan chart in 1380:

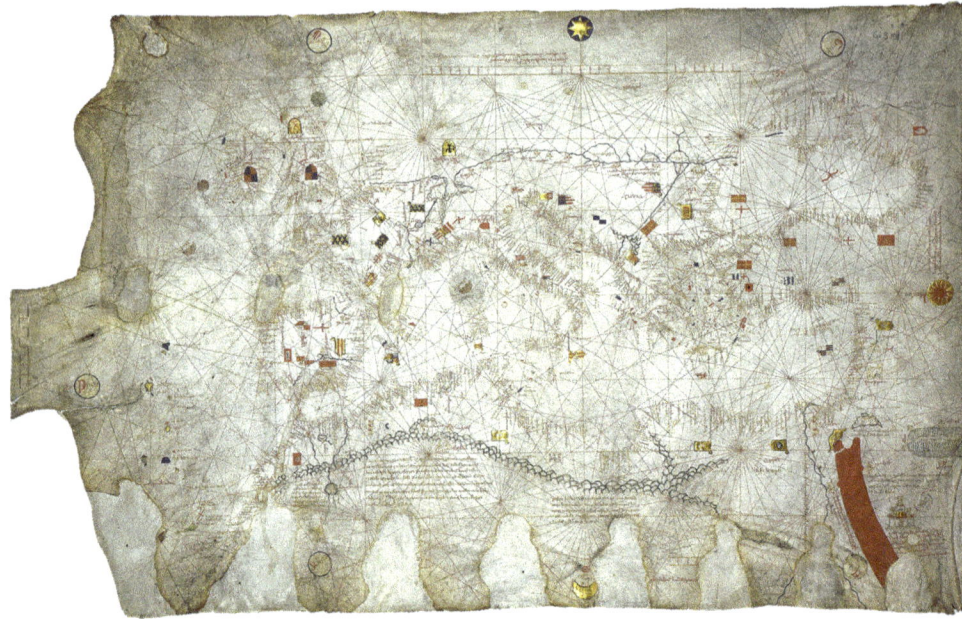

Our attention is drawn to the islands he designed in the Atlantic Ocean.

We notice that "Insulae de Brazil" appeared in three places on the map, as on the Pizzigani brothers map of 1367:

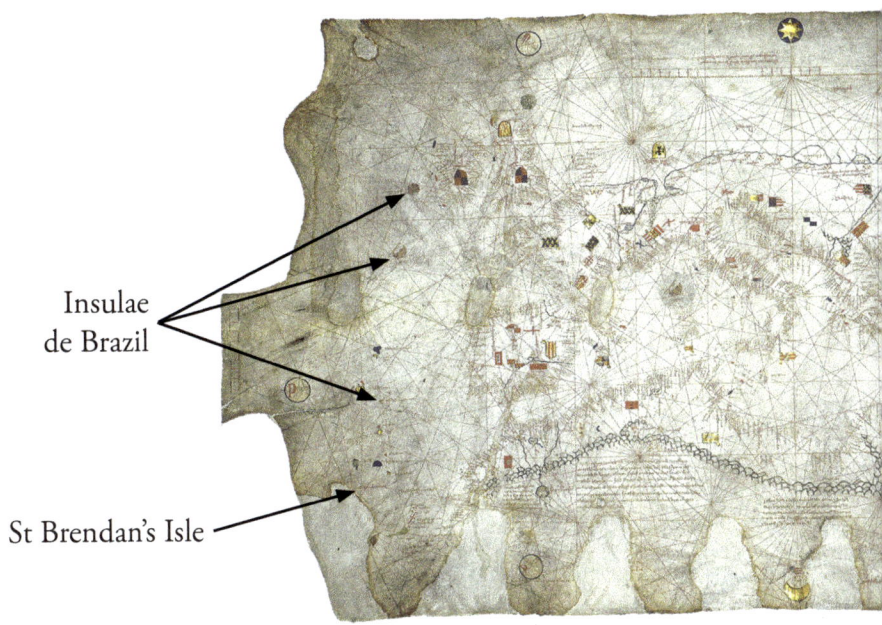

He also made reference to the island of Saint Brendan, but it is not visible, because the map seems to have been damaged there (we positioned it where the inscription appears).

5) Other Appearances of "Brazil"

It should be noted that, well before Christopher Columbus' first voayge, "Brazil" appeared on many other maps and not just the ones drawn by the Majorcan school cartographers. For example, on the Corbitis Atlas, that was designed in Venice at about 1390, i.e. a century earlier:

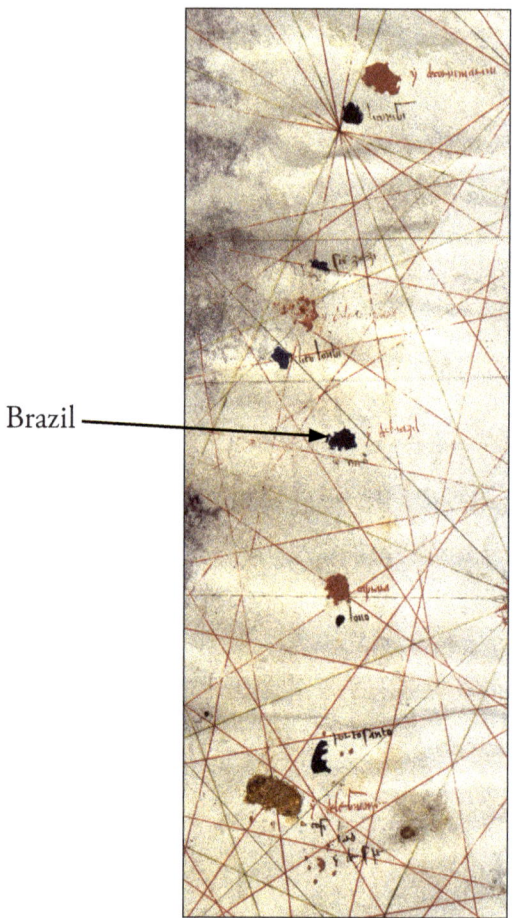

The decades passed by and "Brazil" continued to appear on maps of the Majorcan school, such as in the map of Mecia de Viladestes, in the year 1413. He also drew the "Insola de Brazil" twice, i.e. off the coast of Ireland and southwards in the Atlantic:

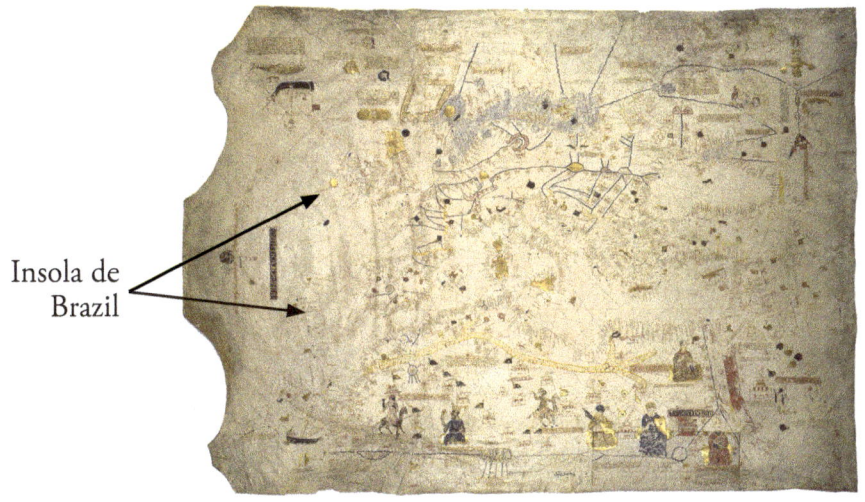

Insola de Brazil

While waiting for the experts to agree on the authenticity of this map, let us add the Viking map of the 13th century, which included the island of "Branziliæ", as we showed in the previous chapter.

If readers desire to go further on this matter, they can search for "Brazil" in all pre-Columbian portolans. This will be a real scavenger hunt.

II. Africa and Australia

Albertinus de Virga, a Venetian cartographer, drew a map on a parchment of 70 by 44 cm (28x17 in), between 1411 and 1415. The world appears as a marked circle:

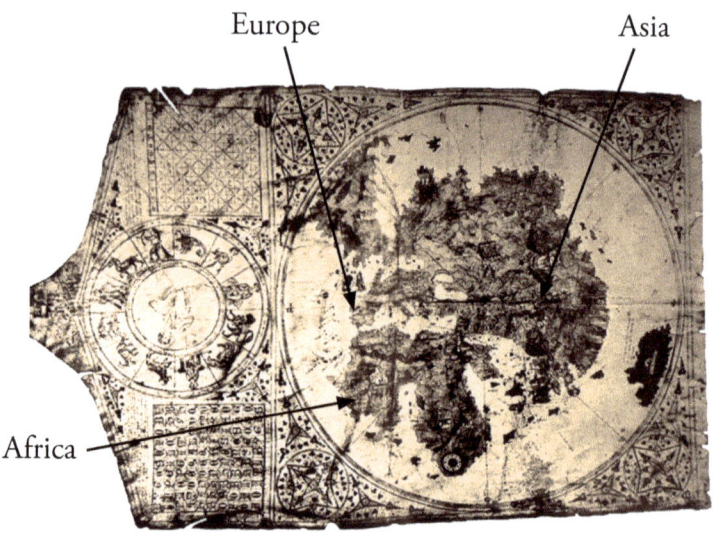

This map raises questions. Firstly, the outline of Africa is pretty well designed, especially the southern half of the continent, although unknown to Europeans at the time. Indeed, it would be another seventy years before Bartholomew Diaz rounded the Cape of Good Hope for the first time and reached the east coast of Africa. Therefore, according to official chronology, it is impossible to precisely represent Africa at that time.

Then, Albertinus de Virga added a large island to the eastern side of his map, just below Asia. It obviously looks like Australia.

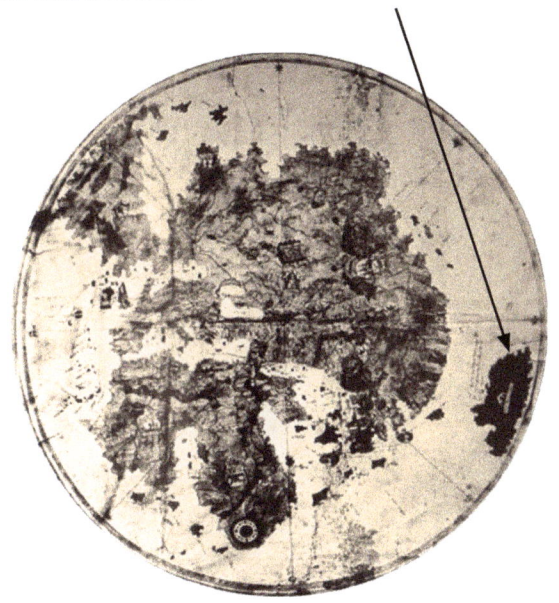

Let us add a satellite image to compare and rotate it:

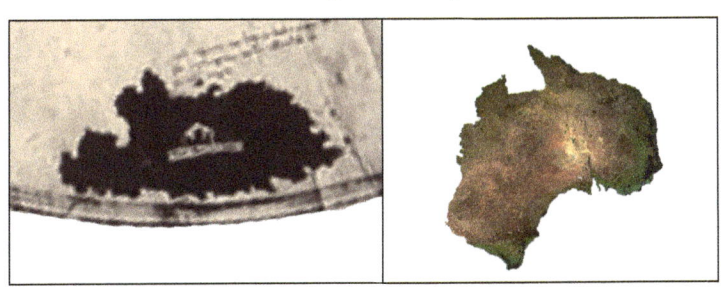

There is little doubt that it was Australia that was drawn. It is even more convincing if we add the bowing of the Earth on the satellite picture, as on the map of Albertinus de Virga:

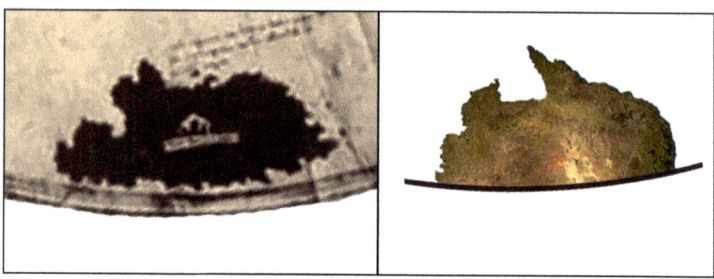

However, Australia was not officially discovered by Europeans until two centuries later, by the Dutch navigator Willem Janszoon in 1606.

Several authors however suggested that the Portuguese were the first Europeans to land in Australia, as early as 1520. It even appeared on the Dieppe maps in the year 1540, i.e. at least sixty years before the discovery of 1606.

Meanwhile, it was more than a century before the supposed arrival of Portuguese in 1520 that Albertinus de Virga drew Australia on his map. So, by what inexplicable miracle did he know the existence and the shape of Australia as early as 1415?

III. The West Indies

Just as with the case of "Brazil," the name "Antilla"[4] appeared on many Pre-Columbian portolans. Hence, Jerald Fritzinger's book *Pre-Columbian Trans-Oceanic Contact*[5] lists about twenty or so:

Maps drawn before 1492 that bear the name "Antilla"	
Zuane Pizzigano	1424
Battista Beccario	1435
Andrea Bianco	1436
Bartolomeo Pareto	1455
Map of Weimar	Around 1460
Grazioso Benincasa	1463
Petrus Roselli	1463
Petrus Roselli	1466
Petrus Roselli	1468
Grazioso Benincasa	1470
Paolo Toscanelli	1474
Cristoforo Soligo	Around 1475
Andrea Benincasa	1476
Albino de Canepa	1480
Grazioso Benincasa	1482
Jacme Bertran	1482
An anonymous Marjorcan map	1487
Albino de Canepa	1489
Martin Behaim / "Erdapfel"	1491-1493

4. The name of the West Indies in languages coming from Latin.
5. *Pre-Columbian Trans-Oceanic Contact*, Jerald Fritzinger, Lulu.com, March 2016.

According to official historians, the name "Antilla" does not imply our current West Indies, but rather the "front islands" or "in front of the known world." Despite their interpretation, this proves that, during the Middle Ages, the presence of islands in the Atlantic and even far beyond the Azores was already known. At this stage, it does not matter if the islands named as "Antilla" represented the West Indies, Cuba or even Brazil, since, in any case, the Arabs had drawn the American continent at least five centuries before the Europeans.

Let us present some of these Portolans wherein the name "Antilia" appears.

Let us present some of these portulans with Antilia. The oldest of them was drawn in 1424 by Zuane Pizzigano, a Venetian cartographer, with islands to the west in the Atlantic:

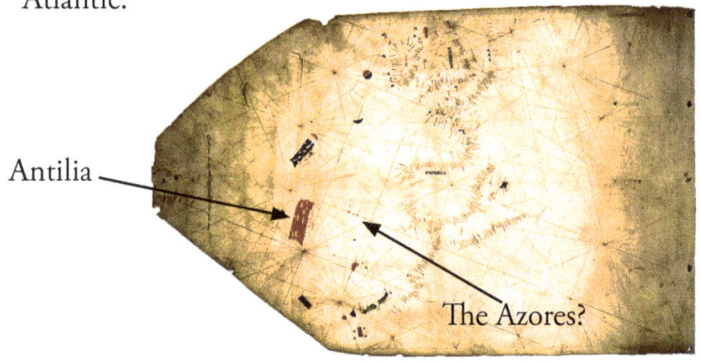

What is strange is that he represented what looks like the Azores, which, however, will be discovered by the Portuguese only a few years later.

Antilia will continue to appear on other maps, like here on Bartolomeo Pareto's map dated 1455:

Then it appeared on Benincasa's map in 1476. He even added the island of Bracil:

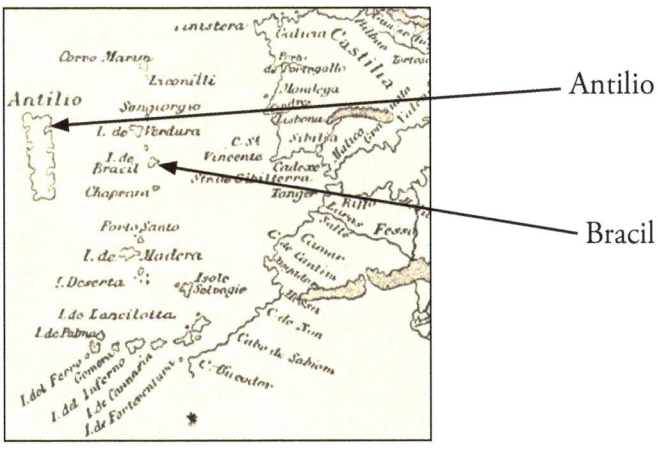

Antilio

Bracil

Martin Behaim was a German navigator born in Nuremberg in 1459. He built a terrestrial globe between 1491 and 1493, measuring fifty centimeters in diameter. He called it "Erdapfel." Here is how it looked:

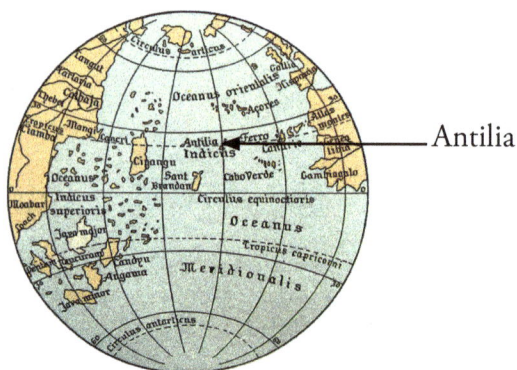
Antilia

The reproduction clearly shows that Martin Behaim did not know the discovery of the New World, as it does not appear on his globe. On the left, there is Asia, on the right, Europe and Africa.
Again, to the West of Africa, almost at the center of the ocean, appears an island called "Antilia."
Saint Brendan's Island was located further south, to the East of Japan, called "Cipangu."

Then came 1492 and Christopher Columbus. It is hard to believe that he never heard of the islands of Antilla, Brazil and Saint Brendan before his first voyage, as they appear on Western maps for over a century and a half, without speaking of the Arab texts and maps.

Chapter 7

After the Discovery of the New World

Finally, America is officially discovered. Yet anomalies continued, as we will see.

1) Piri Reis
Let us start with probably the most well-known map today, which is that of the Turkish Admiral Piri Reis. It was drawn in 1513, but was found in Istanbul only in the year 1929.

This map became famous because many people saw and continue to see information that was not supposed to be known at the time. According to them, it would even be the evidence of the existence of highly advanced ancient civilizations or extraterrestrial visits. For example, the map would describe a part of Antarctica. How can they make such a conclusion? Indeed, South America continues eastward, but not enough to say this is Antarctica.

Antarctica, really?

In addition, if the information came from a superior civilization, the distance of almost a thousand kilometers between the two continents would necessarily be visible:

In comparing the Piri Reis map with other contemporary or later maps, like that of Gerardus Mercator from the year 1596, we notice the same type of error:

It is the same situation for North and Central America, whose representation by Piri Reis is so incorrect that we cannot imagine that the source came from ancient masters or that this map is the image of the Earth as seen from the sky, as resources claim:

(the outline on this map was blackened by us)

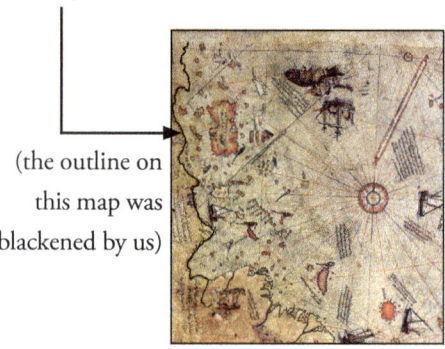

But this map does present a mystery. It is the Spanish writer and journalist Javier Sierra who revealed it in his book *La Ruta Prohibida*. In 2002, he obtained special permission from the Turkish government to view the Piri Reis map.

The specialist accompanying him translated the inscriptions in old Turkish. One text says that the West Indies were discovered in the year 890 of the Arab calendar by a Genoese named Columbus.

But in the Arab calendar, 890 corresponds to 1485, seven years **before** the first official voyage of Christopher Columbus. And Piri Reis added that he received this information from a Spanish prisoner who accompanied Columbus in his first three trips.

Perhaps this is a mistake in the date. It is impossible to know it. Moreover, Piri Reis stated that he used about twenty maps to draw his own, some of which dated back to antiquity. They have all disappeared since then. However, he himself designed many maps of the Mediterranean, which he knew perfectly. Therefore, he did not need a map dating from antiquity to draw it.

Did any of these maps already represented the coast of America? Unfortunately, we will probably never know.

2) Juan de la Cosa

Spanish explorer and cartographer, Juan de la Cosa participated in the discovery of the New World alongside Christopher Columbus, as he was the owner of the *Santa María*, the main ship of the first expedition in 1492. So he drew this map in 1500 as an eyewitness. Historians consider nowadays that this is the first map with America.

What is strange is that Juan de la Cosa seems to represent Cuba as an island, whereas it was seen by Columbus as part of the continent. In addition, the first full tour of Cuba will be made only in 1508, eight years later.

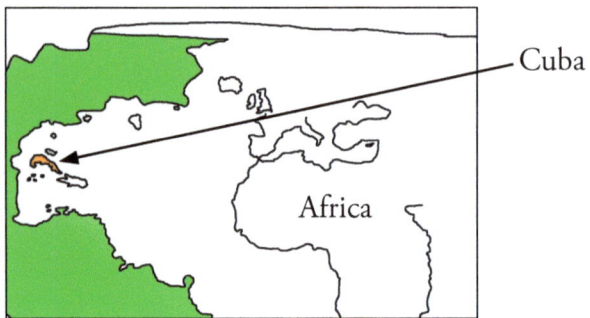

And Bartolomeo Columbus, a brother of Christopher Columbus, commissioned the design of a map in 1506 on which Cuba was absent:

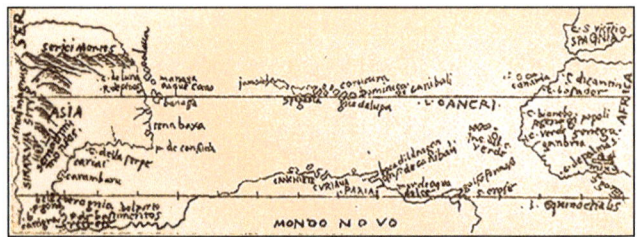

Only South America is the New World, the northern part belongs to Asia. This makes sense, since Christopher Columbus thought he had arrived in India and did not know that he was in America.

3) Pedro Reinel

A Portuguese cartographer born in 1462, Pedro Reinel produced an amazing map in 1504. He certainly knew about the discovery of the New World, but he placed it too far in the north:

Africa

However, he added the island of "Brasil," off Ireland. Thus, twelve years after the first voyage of Christopher Columbus, the link was still not established between South America and this mysterious island of Brazil that has been appearing on maps for almost two centuries.

Eight years later, in 1512, Hieronymus Marini, an Italian architect and military engineer, had understood: he designed what is believed to be the first map with the word "Brasil," though this is not true, as we showed it.

4) Martin Waldseemüller
In 1507 he published a world map, which is amazing for several reasons.
First for its size: 2.30 meters by 1.3 meter (2.1x1.2 y.); it required twelve sheets.
It is also exceptional for the spherical effect of the representation of the Earth.

Then, it is on this map by Martin Waldseemüller that appeared for the first time the name "America." It is a tribute to the navigator Amerigo Vespucci, who sailed far enough south to conclude that this continent was not Asia.

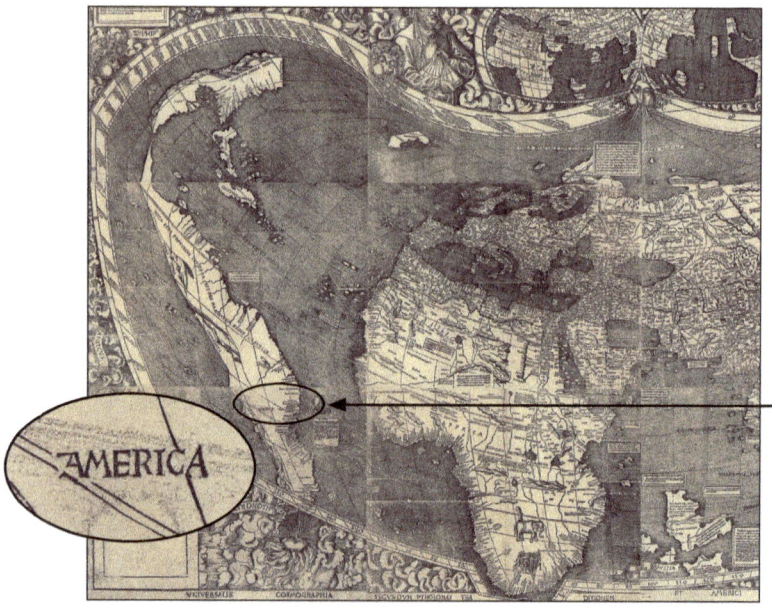

However, something obvious to us but impossible in 1507 is to represent the new continent as separated from Asia. Indeed, it took another six years and 1513 before the Spanish Vasco Núñez de Balboa became the first European to discover the Pacific Ocean, which he called the "South Sea," thirteen years until 1520 before Magellan bypassed the southern tip to reach the Pacific, and until 1741, more than two centuries later, for Vitus

Bering to discover the strait that bears his name, proving that Asia and America were two separate continents.

Furthermore, we saw on page 82 the map that Bartolomeo Columbus had commissioned in 1506, the year just before Martin Waldseemüller delivered his own: only South America is called "New World," the northern part of the continent being Asia. And Bartolomeo Columbus accompanied his brother in "America," whereas Martin Waldseemüller never went there!

Moreover, about sixty years later, in 1565, Paolo Forlani continued to link Asia and North America:

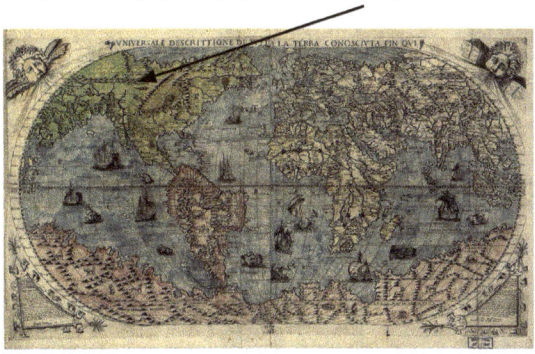

However, Martin Waldseemüller separated the two continents. How could he know this? How could he also have the knowledge that America was made up of two parts? It is indeed impossible to draw it by mere chance or imagination. Since he stayed in France and did not cross the ocean, from which source lost today did he get inspiration? Whatever it may be, the complete tour of the continent had obviously already been completed. But by whom? And at what time?

Although North America designated by the term "Terra ulteri incognita" meaning "faraway unknown land" is small, what is astonishing is that he drew mountains on the western edge of the continent, as if he knew the Rocky Mountains. The coincidence seems impossible. Indeed, why represent mountains in the west and not in the east or in the middle, or even everywhere or not at all? Should we remember that no Westerner is supposed to have already explored or crossed America in 1507?

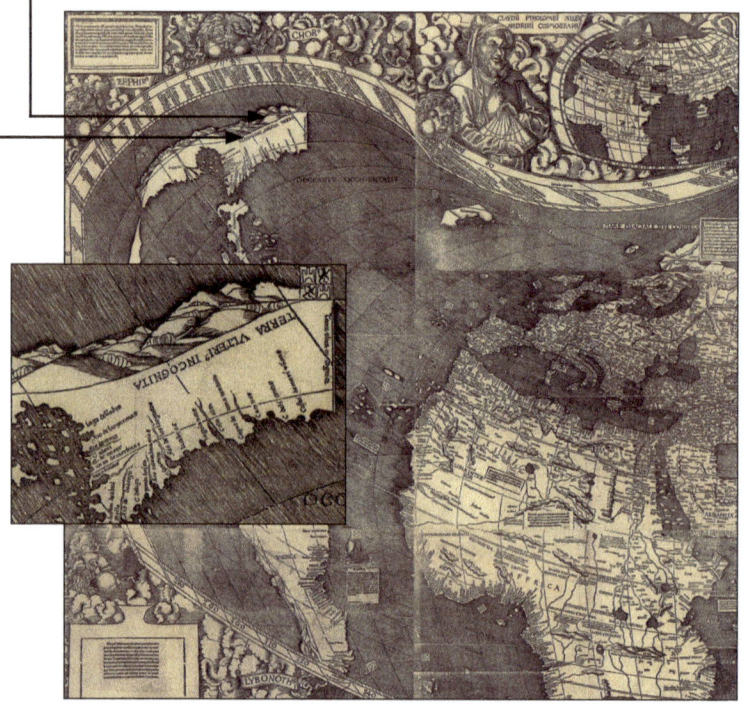

This world map presents other mysteries. The first is India, which does not look like its current form. Instead there is an island called "Taprobana Insula," which some consider to be Ceylon. It is obviously far too large and, moreover, it is surrounded by a multitude of islands, which do not exist or no longer exist.

However, South India, in the time of the ancient Dravida mentioned in the holy book of the Vedas, was an island, which would correspond to the map. But it was thousands of years ago!

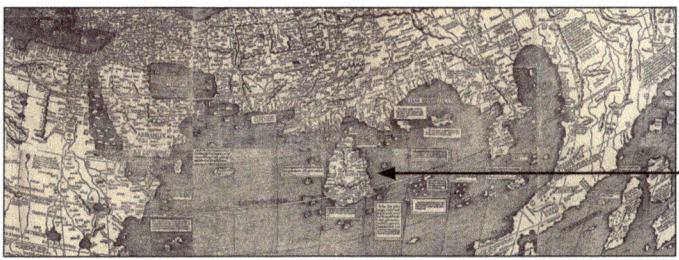

Should we admit that Martin Waldseemüller, as well as most of the cartographers who preceded him since Ptolemy, for almost 1,500 years, drew India as it no longer exist for thousands of years? How is that possible? India had been known in the West for more than two thousand years, and Vasco da Gama arrived by sea nine years earlier (1498), without speaking of Alexander the Great, who conquered part of India in the 4th century BC, or the Greek explorer Scylax of Caryanda, who, at the end of the 5th century BC, was known to have explored the Indus at the request of the Persian emperor Darius I.

Then, as soon as 1502, the Cantino planisphere perfectly represented India:

Yet, forty years later, in 1544, Battista Agnese reproduced quite well the world, including America, but not India, although it had been known and explored for a long time. How is it possible?

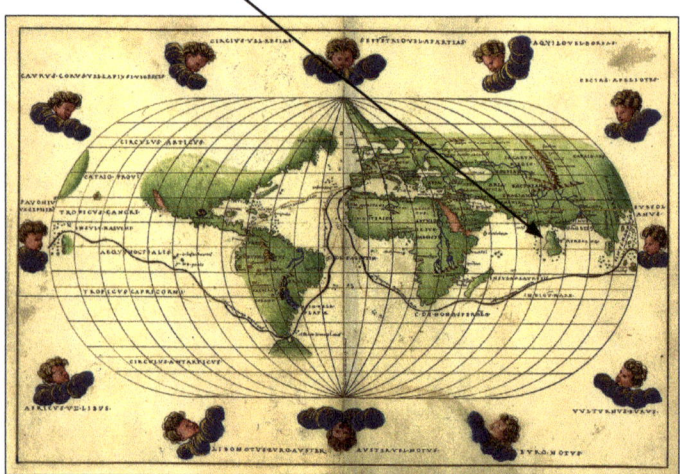

So, let us summarize: Martin Waldseemüller drew America in 1507, which is supposed not to have been explored or even circumvented by anyone, and India the way it was probably thousands of years ago.

Both were impossible in his days. So either the history of discoveries is totally false, which is suggested anyway on the previous maps we have seen, or Martin Waldseemüller had in his possession a map coming from the dawn of time. Obviously, the latter is impossible, because it would mean that it is the official history of mankind which is false.

However, we have not finished with the mysteries of this map. Let us continue the journey. There appears the Bay of Bengal, called "Sinus gangeticus," into which empties the Ganges. On the other side of the Bay of Bengal begins Southeast Asia with the Malay Peninsula, called "Aurea Chersones."

Here is the South China Sea, with the Indochinese peninsula.

This river would be the Mekong, surprisingly well designed.

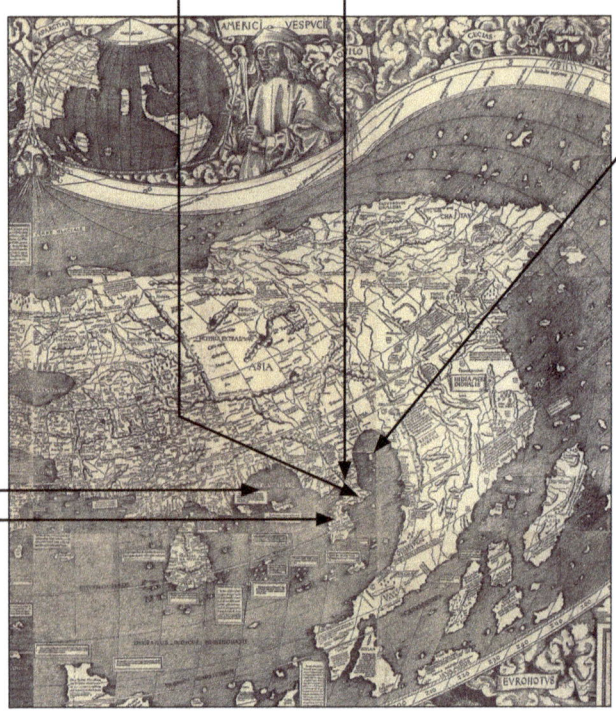

To the east, we reach the Sinus Magnus, which corresponds to the Pacific Ocean. However, on the other side, Martin Waldseemüller widened Asia while adding new land. But what is there in the east of the Pacific Ocean? Of course, America! Therefore, he represented America twice on his map.

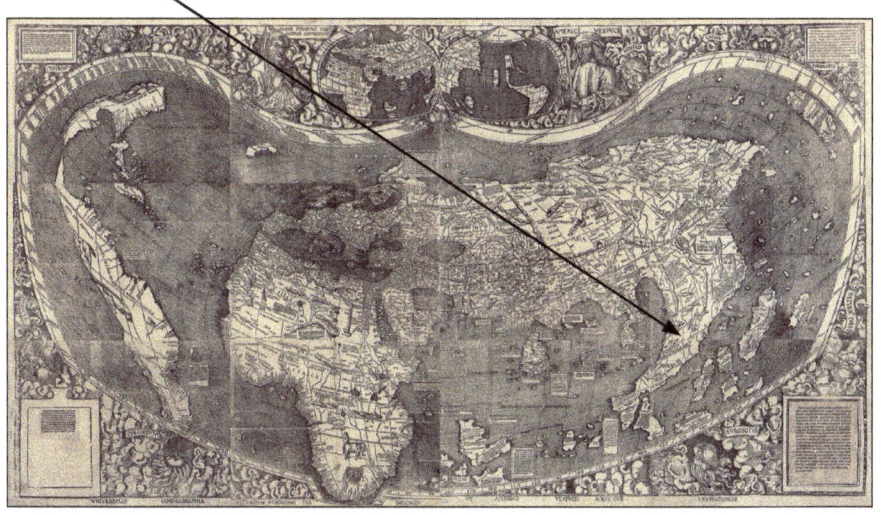

Equally surprising, he gave America, the "true" one, an effect of perspective, as if it were seen from the sky from the Northern Hemisphere.

How could Martin Waldseemüller know the shape of South America? Again, by which map was he inspired?

Maybe by the map of Heinrich Hammer, known as "Henricus Martellus Germanus," a geographer and cartographer from Nuremberg then working in Florence? It dates from 1490-1492, which was fifteen years earlier Martin Waldseemüller's map. This is also one of the last known maps made before Christopher Columbus' first voyage. It would be yet another representation of the world of the time if we did not look at it carefully.

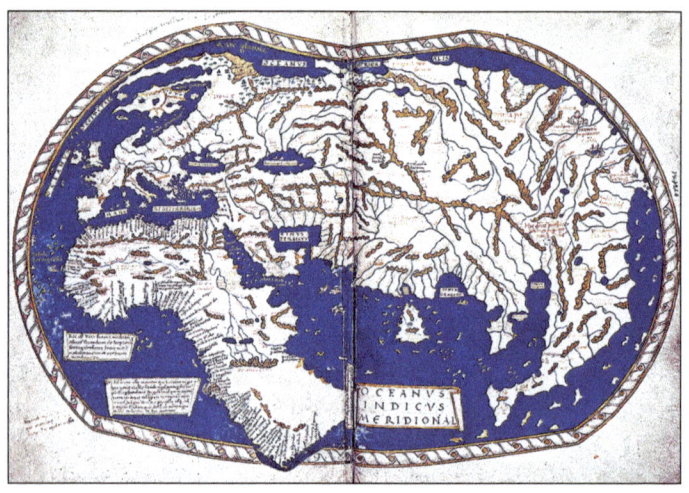

As on Martin Waldseemüller's map, the Bay of Bengal or "Sinus gangeticus" was represented, with the Ganges, then the "Sinus Magnus." We would therefore have South America to the east!

Another element confirms that it could be South America: all rivers located to the east of the continent correspond quite precisely to the rivers of today, while the rivers of Asia do not have the same configuration at all.

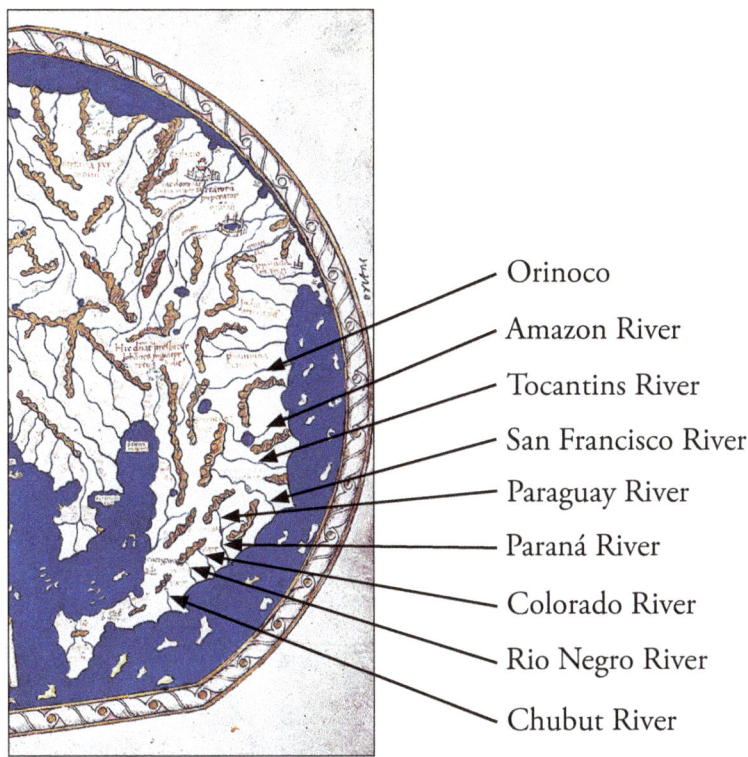

- Orinoco
- Amazon River
- Tocantins River
- San Francisco River
- Paraguay River
- Paraná River
- Colorado River
- Rio Negro River
- Chubut River

Again, how could Henricus Martellus know South America before it was discovered?

It is perhaps the map of Andreas Walsperger, a Benedictine monk and German cartographer of the 15th century, which gives the answer. Designed forty years earlier, in 1450, it is represented in the Arab style, i. e. the South above. Let us present it in the North-South direction:

This strip of land could be Baja California.

The area to the east resembles the American continent, with the southern part here.

This island would correspond to Japan.

But Siberia and Alaska would be connected, as when it was possible to walk from America to Asia. At that time the sea was lower by about one hundred meters (91 y.) and the Bering Strait did not exist yet. But it was at least 12,000 years ago!
Is it reasonable to think that Andreas Walsperger represented the world as it existed 12,000 years ago?

Cartographer Martin Waldseemüller in a 19th century phantasy portrait formerly in the Theatre of Saint-Dié-des-Vosges (France); lost today.
Source: Wikimedia Commons

Chapter 8

Antarctica

We had already mentioned that Antarctica is said to have been officially seen, ("seen," not even explored), for the first time in 1820. However, two French maps of the 16th century totally question the validity of the official chronology.

1) Oronce Finé
A mathematician, astronomer and French cartographer, he lived from 1494 to 1555. Renowned for having produced the first printed map of France, he drew this map of the globe in 1531, the year he was appointed to the chair of mathematics at the Collège Royal, the future College de France:

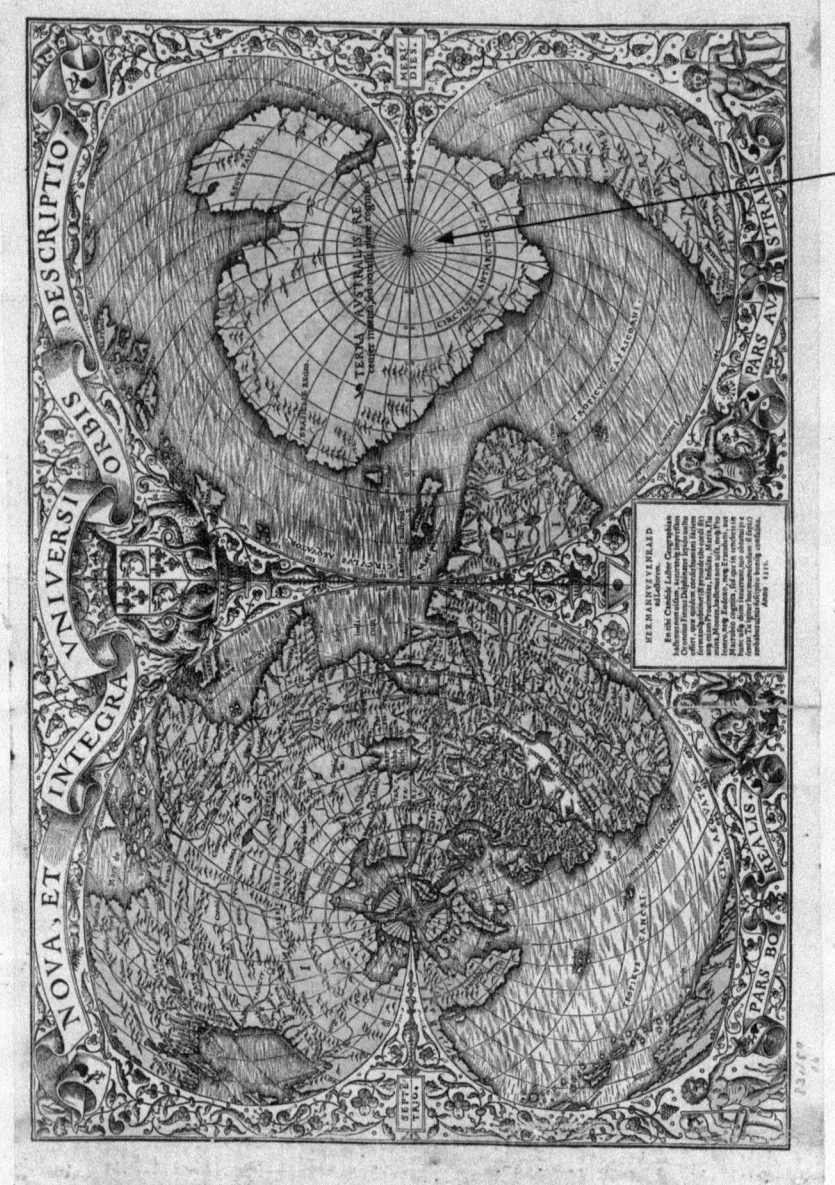

What is immediately striking is the importance on the right of the map of Antarctica, called "Terra Australis." In comparing with a satellite picture of Antarctica, we find that the outlines are similar. How could Oronce Finé draw a continent about which he supposedly did not know since it will only be officially seen for the first time in 1820, i.e. three centuries later?

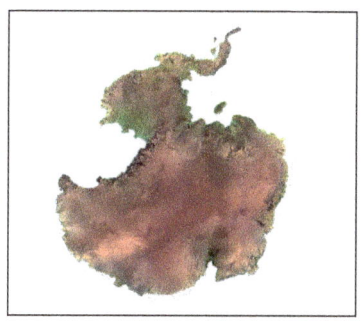

In addition, he added mountains and rivers. Indeed, scientific research confirmed that large rivers flowed in Antarctica but disappeared thousands of years ago, since it was buried under ice.

Oronce Finé had therefore drawn the continent just as it existed thousands of years ago and like no human being was supposed to have ever seen it. How was this possible?

Perhaps he drew rivers and mountains because he did not know that the continent was covered by ice, since he obviously did not go there.

Oronce Finé has maybe represented Australia. Indeed, the shape is similar, but the position does not match. And Oronce Finé added the words "Antarctic Circle." So there is no doubt: it is Antarctica.

Oronce Finé's map remains very mysterious.

2) Jacques de Vaulx

The map in the beautiful book *First Works of Jacques de Vaulx, Driver for The King in the Navy* dating back to 1583 is also mysterious. On this map is represented the Terra Australis, also named "Antarctica." It is therefore not Australia.

The outline resembles Oronce Finé's map but their differences prove that their sources are different.

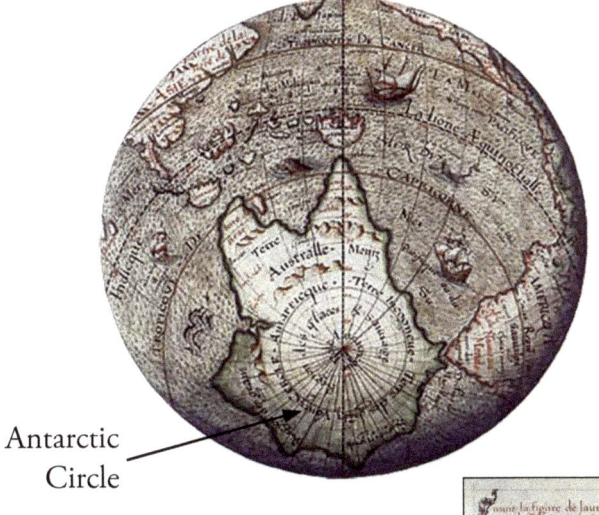

Antarctic Circle

Page of the book

What is even more amazing is that Jacques de Vaulx added the incredible mention "Region of Ice." How did he know that Antarctica was under ice more than two centuries before its discovery?

Furthermore, the map seems to show that only a part of the continent is under ice, which looks even more incredible, as the continent is supposed to be completely covered by it for over 10,000 years.

Region of Ice

So, how can we explain Oronce Finé's and Jacques de Vaulx's maps? At best, we can imagine that they were inspired by older maps. Then, we must admit that men had visited Antarctica in the 16th century, perhaps even before.

"Impossible!", object modern historians.

Oronce Finé's response is the Latin inscription he wrote on his map:

Center inmensa, sed nondum plene cognita

It means:

> "Large center, but not yet fully known."

Yes, we read: "but not yet **fully known**"!

This undoubtedly proves that a part was known, so that Antarctica had already been explored, and at least three centuries before 1820.

But by whom?

By the men of the Middle Ages while this hostile continent was covered by ice? Or by visitors before the ice age, when rivers were still flowing, that is to say thousands of years ago?

This hypothesis implies that these visitors would have drawn maps which were preserved in France until at least the 16th century.

But who, more than 10,000 years ago, could go to Antarctica and draw it precisely, as if it were seen from the sky, respecting the spherical shape of the Earth? The men of Prehistory as they are presented to us?

The mystery becomes even thicker than the Antarctic ice sheet.

Oronce Finé (1494-1555)

Conclusion

At the end of this journey into the heart of ancient maps, a question remains: how could all these cartographers over the centuries represent islands and continents considered unknown and that they did not visit?
And, even more amazing, to have drawn them as they no longer existed for thousands of years?
No one knows. Since they did not go there themselves, the most probable hypothesis is that they had old maps. Obviously, it is impossible to know the source and time of these maps. Then, all hypotheses remain open. One day perhaps, archaeological excavations will reveal one, such as the painting in Nekhen's tomb T100.
Meanwhile, the mystery of ancient maps remains complete. But we now know that our ancestors knew the world better than we think.
Therefore, it is probably becoming urgent to revise our historical knowledge, since the ancient maps prove that the official history of humanity is not quite correct, if not "completely false."

www.ingramcontent.com/pod-product-compliance
Lightning Source LLC
LaVergne TN
LVHW051040070526
838201LV00066B/4867